Memoirs of a Hillbilly Preacher's Daughter
by
Leona Mae

Memoirs of a Hillbilly Preacher's Daughter
Copyright © 2021 by Dr. Phillip E. Copeland

ISBN (978-0-9982704-2-5)

CONTENTS

Introduction

My name is Leona Mae, daughter of a Missouri Ozarks preacher man. Just wanted to share with you all a little bit about my life. I dedicate these memoirs to my two boys Bobby and Dr. Phil and to my only Grandchild Phillip Robert Lamar. I'm so proud of them all and feel so blessed.

French Studio Lebanon   Your Niece Leona Mae

CHAPTER ONE:
MY FAMILY

Andy and Gladys Little in front of the Eureka church.

My parents, Andrew Jackson Little and Gladys Leon Little, were hard working simple people. Dad always said he went to school for eight years and got a third-grade education. I think Mom made it to eighth grade. They did the best they knew how to do with their limited education.

My parents had a total of thirteen children. Dad farmed 160 acres and was a religious minister. I'm sure he didn't become wealthy from any of the churches he pastored. He preached because he loved the Lord and it all came from his heart. He could quote so much of the bible and tried to help all the church members. He preached for nineteen years.

My parents were members of the Eureka Methodist Church. However, Dad preached at several churches, including on occasion Little Vine, a free-will Baptist establishment. Dad would gather the family together before bedtime to read the bible and say prayers.

My Dad's Childhood

My Dad, Andrew (Andy) Jackson Little, was born February 12, 1905 in Niangua, Missouri. His Dad was Perry Covert Little and his Mom was Melissa Bell Mace. When Dad was around four years old, him, his parents, and sister Flossie boarded a train in Niangua, Missouri and travelled to Republic, Missouri to pick strawberries. Dad was given the responsibility of carrying the loose matches in his hand. By the time the train reached Republic, Dad's perspiring hand had ruined the matches. His Dad's chuckle told Dad that even though they needed those matches that it was ok.

Later on when Dad was thirteen years old, the family went to harvest wheat in Kansas. The task given to Grandpa and my Dad was to work on a header barge. Twenty or more horses pulled this monstrous machine. They would steer this big thing along the fields to cut the heads from the wheat. The heads were fed up an elevator to a large wagon until full, afterwards taken to a threshing machine. Dad mentioned he did most the work because his Dad was weak in stature at this time.

My Mom's Childhood

My Mom, Gladys Leon Parscale, was born October 11, 1958 in Dallas County, Missouri. Her Dad was Albert Parscale and her Mom was Oleva Jemes. My Mom had a rough childhood. When she was very young Grandpa Parscale at the age of fifty left my Grandma along with her five children to marry a 19 year old girl by the name of Ruth. He thought he was the cock of the walk. I always suspected he abused Grandma other than emotionally.

Grandma was a tiny woman, only weighing two pounds at birth. Such a small person made her an easy target for Grandpa to beat. She didn't talk right and rumor was among family that Grandpa threw ashes in her face. She breathed the ashes and messed up her voice box.

Anyways Grandma had to give the children to anyone who would take them, feed them and send them to school. Mom ended up staying with Aunt Rachel Miller. I don't know where the brothers and sisters went.

On the other hand, Grandpa Parscale had two kids with his new wife Ruth. They had a son named Carl and a daughter named Hazel. When Grandpa was about to check out of this world he sort of lost his marbles.

I remember when my husband Bob and me went over to Charity, Missouri to visit Grandpa he said, "Ruth fix these people a bed." We cut our visit short when I saw his mind was going and we hadn't planned on spending the night. Ruth lived into her eighties before she passed away in the mid 1990's.

My Dad disliked my Grandpa Parscale so much that he wouldn't even take us kids to go visit him. However, later in life as an adult I did go see him and recognized him as my Grandpa.

My Siblings

My Dad was so hard on us kids and extra protective with the girls. As us kids grew older we could not wait to leave the farm and live a normal life of freedom to make our own decisions whether good or bad.

My oldest brother, James Deryl (J.D.), got through high school when one day he had stolen Dad's wallet and just disappeared from the farm. My parents were so upset and concerned about him. Several weeks passed when a letter I believe came from California. After some time had passed J.D. returned home to the farm. Shortly thereafter he went off to college.

My brother first started off teaching for a few years and eventually attended seminary to become a preacher. He married Leona Crawford who seemed like a homely kind of girl. J.D. served as the pastor for the United Methodist Churches, working his way up the ranks as the District Superintendent that was similar to a bishop for other religious affiliations. Unfortunately, J.D. lost his wife Leona to cancer in 1994. A year later he met Violet Davis and married again.

Then there was my next eldest brother, Jackie, who we always called Jack. He and Dad did not click well at all so Jack ended up leaving the farm at around 14 years old. Unlike J.D. he never returned back home. Jack migrated to Oklahoma where he met some good people. Among these people was Carol who he fell in love with and married.

Jack and his new wife moved to New Mexico where they had six children together and prospered. Following in his Dad's and older brother's footsteps, Jack became a Christian minister. He was also an entrepreneur as a car sales owner.

He got his pilot license and began flying his little plane overseas to other countries such as Haiti, Russia, and the Philippines for missionary work to spread the Christian word. Jack had a natural talent to find ways to make money and would bring back artifacts to the states for a lucrative profit. During this time Jack also prospered at his car dealership back in New Mexico. Many of his auto sales were south of the border to Mexicans. They seemed to love especially the pickup trucks Jack sold to them.

Misfortune struck again and Jack lost his wife Carol who was only 47 years old. She was diabetic. Jack eventually met Judy and married her. She was a big help to Jack in his business. Neither J.D. nor Jack liked to be alone and they were both fortunate to find happiness with their second marriages.

News from Church

Former resident travels to Moscow to deliver God's word

The following article was written by Dave McDonald of the Cibola County (N.M.) Beacon. It is about former Marchfield resident Jack Little, who recently traveled to Moscow, and is reprinted with permission of the Beacon.

by Dave McDonald
of the Beacon staff

Jack Little was just like any other visitor at Lenin's Tomb in Moscow — well, not quite.

Most of them are Russians, of course, and most of them don't pass out copies of the New Testament to the elite Soviet Guard there.

But Little did.

The Milan (N.M.) auto dealer was one of a half-dozen Americans who recently spent nearly two weeks in the Soviet Union doing missionary work in the country that until two years ago and for nearly three-quarters of a century was officially atheist.

"Sometimes, in Moscow, the snow gets six to eight feet deep and stays there three to four months at a time," Little said.

And he describes the average Soviet in one word — friendly.

"I was always led to believe they were hostile. And they were led to believe we were hostile."

And the Soviet government was very cooperative, he recalled, providing a Greyhound-sized bus for Little, his five fellow missionaries and their interpreter.

With four of them from Missouri and one from Kansas, Little was

JACK LITTLE

the only New Mexican in the entourage.

They visited and preached at Gus Crystalian, a factory town about 100 miles east of Moscow. As its name indicates, the city's main industry is the manufacturing of lead crystal, which Little described as "very beautiful, artistic and well-crafted."

And the town and its citizens weren't all that exotic, he said.

"If I were to pick you up and put you down right in the middle of Gus Crystalian, you'd think you were in a typical factory town in the Midwest, USA," Little said.

But, he recalled, there are differences. Private residences are rare, almost unheard of, he said. In their place are huge apartment complexes, a block square and 30 to 40 stories high.

In some cases, Little reported, 20 families will share one kitchen with its single stove and refrigerator.

Most food comes in sacks, he

said, such as a sack of potatoes or a sack of cabbage. And the average Russian doesn't have all that much meat in his diet that requires refrigeration.

Since everything is subsidized by the government, prices are below bargain level. A Big Mac, an order of fries and a medium Pepsi-Cola at the McDonald's in Moscow cost Little 20 cents in U.S. money.

And some of the evangelists, delivering New Testaments, were flown 4,000 miles roundtrip on an Aeroflot jetliner — fare per passenger, $3.

And that was the focus of the trip, to spread the Word, literally, a task Little sees as just beginning and very necessary.

He passed out 1,700 New Testaments in Gus Crystalian.

The trip and the scriptures were part of a project of Overseas Evangelism Ministries of Joplin, Mo., the Bible League of Lakeview, Mo., and Revival Fire Ministries.

The latter group has an agreement with the Soviet government to deliver a half-million New Testaments to be used as supplementary textbooks in Russian schools.

A 40-cent donation purchases a New Testament to be delivered to the Russians, Little said.

"All that money goes only for Bibles," he told the Beacon, with none for administrative costs or even transportation.

Free passage for John Todd of Revival Fires and for shipments of scripture is being provided by the German airline Lufthansa.

King Crossword	Word Play
ACROSS	IRREMEDIABLE — impossible to remedy, corr...

My brother Jack when he was flying around doing God's work.

My oldest sister and second oldest sibling, Mary, helped out with the cooking and loved to sew. Just like Mom had done making our dresses, Mary made her own dresses out of feed sacks and even wore her homemade dresses when going off to college.

Mary became a teacher and soon thereafter met a Baptist Minister by the name of Harry Foley. They fell in love and were married. That would make four preachers in the family so far.

The next older brother was Howard. He was the outgoing one. So handsome, tall, wavy dark hair and a gold crown on a front tooth. Howard owned a car while he was in high school and would take me places with him. He dated several girls. One stands out in my memory, her name was Betty Lou. She was short, sort of chubby and was big breasted. Howard called her Titty Love.

After Howard graduated high school, he moved to Wichita, Kansas where he got a good job with Beech Aircraft. It was there that he met a real short woman Essie Mae. She also had a good job with Boeing Aircraft. Essie was primarily of French blood. She wore tight fitting jeans and smoked. Howard was madly in love with Essie so he came rushing home with her after only knowing her three weeks.

Howard approached Dad to sign papers so he could marry Essie. Dad said, "Well, I'll sign Howard, but you have a long time to regret doing this." And believe me, our Dad knew a lot about the appearance of someone and their character.

Essie and Howard did really well together for the first few years. They bought a new house, new car, and new furniture. They had a daughter Vickie and then a son Rickie came along. Then two more sons Eddie and Shawn followed. Poor little Vickie did so much of the caring for her little brothers. Her Mom Essie didn't cook or keep house very well.

Howard started running around with women and Essie soon followed the same pattern. Ended up being a big mess. One of his women was Barbara. While Howard was at her house one night, her husband unexpectedly came home. So Howard left his boots behind and dropped out of the window. Howard had told me himself about this incident.

A short time later my next older brother Don who was three years older than me had also moved to Wichita after he graduated high school. Funny enough he began to date the same Barbara that my brother Howard had messed around with when she was married. I guess she divorced her husband and married

Don who thought he made a good catch but that could be a matter of opinion.

Howard and his kids.

Anyways Dad may have been pretty accurate with his reservations about them getting married in the first place. Howard and Essie did indeed regret their marriage and eventually split up. Howard moved in with Chloctta Buttram at Rader which wasn't really a town, it just had a country store with a hand full of folks by the last name of Rader living around it. A population of less than double digits.

By this time Howard was on Social Security disability as the result of a car accident sometime before this. He had a head on collision one night and I went rushing down to where he was at St. John's Hospital in Springfield, Missouri. My poor brother's head was swelled up as big as a dish pan. I really didn't see how he would survive.

Howard had a Chinese Surgeon by the name of Dr. Tsong who was supposed to be good. Well, he really lived up to his reputation. The good doctor did brain surgery and pulled off a miracle. Dr. Tsong told Dad that some of his son's brain was so damaged and had to throw it away. Howard always acted so crazy before the accident so we didn't see much change after.

The Little family (Front row left to right: Glenn, Wayne, Andy, Gladys, Robert, Ann, Jean. Back row left to right: Mary, Grace, Jack, Howard, Don, J.D. Perry, Leona)

And if the brain damage wasn't enough, Howard was on medication for lifelong treatment of a heart attack he had at a very young age. I guess the disability benefits were from both the heart and brain situations. I don't think he ever supported his four children. Howard just bought liquor and maybe paid for his keep at Chloetta's out of his disability checks.

Well, one day Howard was going to drive down to Arkansas to visit his children and he got a motel room at Marshfield, Missouri the night before he was to head that way. He had a suitcase full of liquor and at the same time he had to take his heart medication. The two didn't mix so they found his dead body four days later in his motel room. So long that we had to have a closed casket at the funeral.

My Grandparents

My Grandparents on my Dad's side, Perry Covert and Melissa Bell Little, lived a short distance from our log cabin. Grandma Bell was the seventh child of twelve children born February 19, 1878 in Greene County, Tennessee to Andrew Jackson Mace and Ester (Easter) Lavina Keesling. She married Grandpa Perry March 14, 1900 in Webster County, Missouri. My Dad's great Grandfather, George Keesling, was the son of Jacob Keesling and Catherine Phillippi who originally came from Dresdan, Saxony, Switzerland in 1704. They came over to America in 1749.

Just some interesting family history about Grandma Bell's Grandma, Hannah (Parks) Keesling. Our ancestor Andrew Parks married Harriet Washington at Baltimore, Maryland in 1796. She was the daughter of Samuel Washington who was a colonial American officer and politician and was also the brother of George Washington, our first President. Samuel was a Colonel in the Virginia Militia and afterwards served as a parish vestryman. He was later appointed as a Justice and then was the Sheriff of Stafford County, Virginia.

Anyways, I remember Grandma Bell would go down to the well and draw water to wash clothes on the washboard. She scrubbed for hours while humming gospel hymns. Grandma would bake cookies that filled the air with an aroma tempting us to sneak a cookie before Grandma even finished cooking. Occasionally I may pinch a little bit of cookie dough out of the bowl, chewing even after it disappeared in my mouth. I remember how Grandpa Perry would clean my fingernails with his pocketknife. I dread the good job he did as he grinded away.

Neither of my grandparents were of a very healthy stature. Grandpa Perry struggled through his back pain. In fact, I never saw him walk without holding on to the wall or furniture for support. Grandpa died of old age. Grandma Bell suffered from diabetes which seemed to cause some problems with her legs and feet. It was ultimately gangrene in her heel that took her life. Nowadays her death would have been prevented with the amputation of her foot or lower leg.

My only aunt, Flossie Jinks, took care of both my Grandparents until my Grandma's death. At such time Grandpa moved in with us and we all took care of him until his passing. Aunt Flossie lived a long life until her death at the ripe old age of 95. Aunt Flossie had two daughters, Nola and Marjorie and one son, Bill.

Marjorie was closest to my age and would spend the night with us. We really dreaded those nights because Marjorie seemed to always wet the bed. However, we were never allowed to spend the night with anybody else, whether they were school pals or cousins. Dad especially didn't trust anyone around us girls so we were heavily protected.

Some of My Other Relatives

We did not work on Sundays except to milk cows. Dad said this was the Lord's day of rest. So we would always go to church Sunday mornings and in the afternoons we would go visit relatives. We would go visit Dad's only sister Flossie Jinks and her husband uncle Ed.

Us kids would love eating up their graham crackers, a treat we never had at our house. That made it so much more of a special treat we really enjoyed. We would grab up any of the newspapers they had laying around from that week which was also delivered on Sunday. But Dad wouldn't let us read the funnies section until Monday. I guess he thought it would corrupt our minds on the Lord's day.

Great Uncle Will and Aunt Betty Mace lived on a farm that joined our land. They were very conservative people. Aunt Betty chewed tobacco and used a coffee can as a spittoon. She had a real small neck, it would remind me of Olive Oil on Popeye.

Our Family Tree

Our family name "Little" was spelled "Littel" in Hibaldstow, Lincolnshire County, England in late 1600's when Robert Littel and Ann were born. Their children were Robert, Thomas, and Mary. They are buried in Hibaldstow Parish Cemetery. The son Robert married Elizabeth Cowder March 6, 1734. They had three children: Ann, Thomas, and Mary.

Their son, Thomas, married Ann Hunt May 22, 1764. They also had three children: Thomas, Robert, and Diana. Their son, Thomas, married Mary Bulivent June 16, 1813. As the pattern seems to be, they also had three children: Ann, Elizabeth, and Robert. Their son, Robert, married Mary Ann Spensley in Yorkshire, England.

Robert and Mary (Spensley) Little were my great great Grandparents who left England and sailed to Canada in 1848.They only had one child, Thomas Howard, at that time. They had six more children after they moved to North America. Their firstborn, Thomas, was my great Grandfather who is buried in Eureka Cemetery, Webster County, Missouri.

My great Grandfather Thomas was five years old when they came over to America. He recalled that the ship was powered with a steam engine as well as sails. One day during their journey, he wandered around the ship and up to where the Captain was situated. He said the Captain put five spoonfuls of sugar in his coffee.

When their family arrived in Canada they settled down and were farmers for seven years. Then they moved on down to Yates County, New York to continue farming. My great great

Grandfather Robert made several trips back to England after his arrival to America in 1848.

On August 11, 1862, when Thomas was eighteen years old he enlisted in the Union Army, Company B, 148th, New York Infantry. His regiment was assigned to the Army of the James, in Virginia under General Benjamin Butler. Thomas was in a number of important engagements, among them being Cold Harbor, Petersburg, and others.

However, he was a rather frail man and could not withstand the hardships of war. He spent a lot of time in the hospital, being in one at Portsmouth for eleven months. Thomas was discharged from military service January 25, 1865 in Richmond, Virginia. He returned to farming in New York at that time. Thomas farmed and worked in a sawmill for eight years.

Thomas met Hannah M. Covert from Steuben County, Painted Post, New York and they got married December 30, 1869. A few years later in 1873 they moved to Allegan County, Michigan to continue farming. The land there was very fertile, a deep black soil deposited by ancient glaciers. The glacier deposited large boulders in a few places and left lakes.

My great Grandparents had seven children: Anna, Arthur Earnest, Lizzie, Perry Covert (my Grandfather), Glenn Howard, Irving Stanley, and Grace Bell. My Grandfather Perry Covert Little was born July 12, 1877 in Allegan County, Michigan.

Great Grandfather Thomas was a Republican and cast his first vote for Abraham Lincoln. His religious belief was of the Second Adventists faith. You could say this faith was a big bowl of Seventh Day Adventist, Methodist, and Baptist religions all stirred up into one.

My great Grandparents Thomas and Hannah Little moved from Michigan to Nebraska in 1892, purchasing a farm in Phelps County. There was very little rain there and no existing irrigation. It was 1896 when it became evident that the Littles could no longer survive in this dry region. They packed up and moved to Webster County, Missouri. My great grandparents purchased 160 acres of land in the Eureka community of Rader.

CHAPTER TWO:
MY CHILDHOOD

It was after the great depression that I came into this world. On May 3, 1938, I was born in a two-room log cabin tucked away in the woods of our Ozark farm in Webster County, Missouri. I was child number six of twelve brothers and sisters.

Copperhead snakes lived underneath the log cabin. Dad could smell their odor and once in the night Dad woke up and shot one that had gotten into the cabin. Despite growing up with these snakes all over the farm, we were never bitten.

We would walk from the log cabin to Church at Eureka. I don't remember Dad having a car there. I think I had a health problem back then. When we had to cross fences I would have to rest awhile as I felt weak. Doctors were only contacted when a new baby was about to arrive. I do remember we had a bottle of red medicine used for all of our cuts and wounds.

New House

In 1943, I remember when Dad built a new two-bedroom house on the side of our farm closest to the gravel road passing our acreage. The six-room house was like a mansion compared to the two-room log cabin. The new home had a girls bedroom, a boys bedroom, a kitchen, a living room, a kitchen, storage room, front open porch, and back closed end porch. And since indoor bathrooms were unheard of at this time Dad had built an outhouse.

I was about 5 years old when we moved from the log cabin to our brand new house that Dad built. Dad had built his own log sawing mill where he cut all the logs into the lumber used for building the new house. This big and tall hard working man would carry the stone found on our land to be used for the foundation, siding, and porches.

Dad never seemed to finish anything that he started to build which included our new house. The rock siding was left unfinished until the day he died. I guess he was just so overwhelmed with working the land, building the barn, the chicken house, the multiple sheds, and the house just to name a few things.

Andy and Gladys Little in front of the new house he built.

I was quite responsible for my age so they had me carry the match box across the hills on our journey to the new home. The house smelled so new with fresh wood and stone. There weren't any windows yet but we were so anxious to move in.

I don't know how us kids ever managed with only one bedroom for all us girls and one for all the boys. We tried to sleep both ways on the bed but our feet would always seem to get cold.

Mom and Dad didn't even have a bedroom. They slept in the living room with their bed tucked into the far front corner of the room next to the front door.

The woodburning stove was located in the opposite corner of the room right before you go into the kitchen area. This was considered the center of the house and the best place to have the fire burning during the cold winter days.

My youngest brother Robert on his motorcycle in front of the house on the farm.

Any of the babies would sleep with Mom and Dad until they were finished nursing. The only exception was the youngest sibling, my brother Robert. Mom had him when she was 45 years old. Robert was spoiled rotten and slept with them until he was 12 years old. I always said Mom was too old when she had him and that was what was wrong with Robert.

I think Robert was still a teenager when Dad was stricken with lung cancer. I was 34 at the time and never seen my Dad smoke. However, he did smoke when him and Mom were first married. Mom tried hiding or throwing away his cigarettes but Dad would always go buy some more. I guess it caught up to him.

Where Babies Came From

My parents were real hush hush about sex and about where babies came from. They told my siblings and me that our country doctor, Dr. Lindsay, would bring the babies in the black doctor bag he carried. Over the years us kids wondered why Mom would lay in the bed for two or three weeks just moaning a lot. Then our parents told us the cows found baby calves under tree stumps. Being curious, we would walk all over the farm looking for stumps turn upside down and found nothing. That really messed with our minds.

Of course, in actuality Dr. Lindsay came from the small rural town of Conway to deliver each of us, along with the assistance of one of our neighbor ladies. My Mom struggled in pain throughout each birth without even an aspirin.

Farm Life

Dad woke up way before the rooster crowed and began grilling up the meat for breakfast. When the meat was done he would wake up Mommy to come make some biscuits. They finished cooking around 5 in the morning when Dad would wake up us kids to eat. We would eat and then hiked over to the barn where we would milk the cows. We sometimes would find the cows laying down in their own manure and their udders were filthy. This was the area where we had to squeeze on the cow's tits to get the milk.

I learned how to milk cows by hand when I was ten years old. The barn was only half built and full of cracks so in the winter time we would nearly freeze to death trying to milk. Wind and snow would gust through the cracks that often numbed my hands and body.

Here are some of the Holstein cows we milked back on the farm.

I remember this one mean ole cow named Turvy. If any of us walked behind her she would kick with both her hind legs with every intent to hurt us. Dad had to put some kickers on her. Finally when Dad was fed up with Turvy, he took the mean ole cow to the sale barn for auction.

All us kids still living at home and were old enough were assigned certain cows to milk both morning and night. Don had to milk a huge Roan cow. We named her Roany. She only had three udders, two were normal but the third was very big. You either had to strip it or use both hands.

Don felt responsible that he was assigned to milk Roany but he didn't feel like messing with her so he hired me to milk this one. I could handle Roany just fine. Sometimes she would kick but I grabbed her leg and forced her to put it back down. However, I seemed to always have to remind Don when to pay up for my cow milking services.

Before Dad got a corn planter there were probably six or seven of us kids old enough and responsible enough to drop the corn by hand down all the long rows, feeling like we would never finish planting.

My oldest sister Mary wasn't much of a work horse. She would get tired and dump all of her corn seed at the end of one of her assigned rows. She thought she was getting rid of it but somehow the corn still sprouted and grew regardless of how its planted. Dad did pinpoint it out to Mary what she had done. I don't remember her getting punished. A matter of fact, Mary didn't even have to go out into the field to plant the following year.

When Dad found the time he would build up brush piles to burn and clear off a lot of the farm all by himself. Then in the Fall on a still night we would all go over and help Dad keep the brush fire under control. I would take a few of those molasses cookies along. They were big as flying saucers.

During there were different things Dad had to do and needed the help of the older boys. So on one occasion he needed sprouts cut and gave several boys a mattock to cut them down with. Dad went back to check on how much the boys got done and they were all gone. He found them at the river. The boys wanted to swim instead of cutting sprouts.

Dad didn't want us girls to do the heavy lifting so he would only have the boys do those type of chores such as unloading the big feed sacks or hauling hay bales. He just didn't think it was a good idea. However, I did lift a 100-pound bag of feed just to see if I could do it. I reckon I was pretty strong for a girl and maybe a lot of boys. I could hold my own.

Dad would bale the hay into 80 to 120 pound bales that would be left in rows out int the field. Then the boys would go out to the field and load up the bales onto a wagon pulled by the tractor. One of us girls or smaller boys would drive the tractor while the bigger boys walked along the wagon to buck the hay bales onto the wagon while it moved along the rows. They would then haul the hay to the barn and unload.

On back of the hay wagon.

Sometimes the boys liked to catch snakes and hide them between the bales of hay on the wagon. When they got to the barn they would scare us girls with the snakes. I remember one day Howard chased a Blue Racer snake and it crawled right up a tree. So he climb right up the tree and start shaking the limbs. The snake tumbled out of the tree and landed around Howard's neck, In total shock he just dropped to the ground and rolled around to get away from the snake. I don't think he ever tried that stunt again.

We did our blackberry picking over at my Great Uncle's farm which joined ours. We picked berries for several days and shared the with the Mace's in order to get enough to take us through the Winter. Of course, we had ticks, chiggers, and snakes to cope with. And the green snakes blended in with the vines. One of those snakes fell into Mary's bucket. She abruptly dropped it and went home. Mary had enough that day. The boys didn't seem to mind snakes, they rather enjoyed them. They would either take to play tricks with the girls or they would just kill them and bring them home.

Plowing the rows in the fields.

So one day my sister Grace and I went to pick gooseberries over in the hollow. We found a vine and started picking the berries. All of a sudden we heard a rustling in the leaves nearby and glanced over. To our surprise it was two whip snakes. Little did we know about sex, but now I suppose those snakes were making love. They were all tangled together and I mean they were some big snakes. Their lower bodies about halfway were red underneath.

Grace and I thought we would kill the snakes and take them home to brag to our brothers. We were about a mile from our house. Dad had always warned us about Whip snakes. They were supposed to be real mean, though not deadly like the copperheads. He always told us those snakes would whip us to death. So if we were ever faced with a situation of protection against them we should get by a tree and they would go away.

That old barn sure was cold in the winter time with the cold wind blowing through all the cracks.

Grace and I were getting all prepared for our ordeal. We found a big stick to carry them home on so we were ready now for the big job. We thought we needed to get the snakes separated since they were still love making. So we threw rocks at them and believe me they got done and started chasing us. Grace left her berries and bucket there. We both ran fast as we could down through the alfalfa field. I was ahead of Grace and I looked back, both snakes had their heads up in the air and after us.

Somewhere the snakes got tired and stopped. Maybe they decided it was more fun to make love than to chase two Little girls. I wasn't about to find a tree like Dad said. We were about a half a mile from any tree. We never tried that again. We were a couple of scared kids and not enough berries for a pie.

View of the farm with the chicken coop to the right and the barn in the distant background.

Looking back on the farm life I realize even more how hard it was growing up. We were less like kids and more like farm hands. We made things fun with what we had. Creating our own little drama and adventures really helped get through the difficult times as a kid on the Little farm.

Elementary School

There were no school buses back then so we had to hike about a mile to the little school building. We all attended a two room, two teacher school named Eureka. One room had grades one through four and the other room had grades five through eight. We had outhouses instead of indoor bathrooms back then.

I remember one of the two teachers, Clovis Vestal, smoked so in order to do it privately he would walk out to the outhouse when he needed a cigarette. All of us students would smell the smoke and knew what he was doing but acted like we didn't know.

The other teacher was my cousin Kenneth Lee. I made good grades and learned a lot in elementary school. I always thought Kenneth graded us high because we were relatives but we were all good spellers. The teachers would comment, "We know they're a Little cause they can spell so good." I made the highest grades throughout the school years.

We had to bring our own lunches to school back then and believe me we took whatever Mom had the ingredients to cook. Biscuits she made out of sour milk. Having all the cows milk available at times we just spread butter between a biscuit.

Food on Our Table

My parents were able to feed the whole family and made money off the farm land and animals. We had plenty of homemade butter, but my parents didn't have any fancy churns to put it in. So we would pour the cream into gallon jars and shake them until they made butter. I didn't mind that job. We made cottage cheese. Mom and Dad had a cream separator. Seems as though we got more money from the cream we sold than selling the milk. When us kids milked the cows we would squirt milk from the cow's tits to our cats, at least until Dad caught us.

We didn't have deep freezers back then either so we had to put everything in canning jars. I remember when we would butcher hogs. Dad would heat up a big barrel of water to boiling and use hot gunny sacks to lay over the hogs. Us older kids would have to use a sharp knife to scrape the hair off the hogs. Then when we got all that done Dad would put the hams in the smokehouse. We sugar cured the bacon and would always eat the liver first since Dad could easily get to that first.

We cut up a lot of the meat, ground it up to make sausage. We fried the sausage balls and stuffed into the jars, pouring the hot grease over them until the jars were full. All of the canning jars were placed carefully on end in our cellar under the house.

All of the meats were so good. Dad would always save one ham for Easter Sunday breakfast. Us kids took turns walking down to the chicken coop to gather all the eggs they lay for the day. We would always see how many eggs we could eat at Easter breakfast. Dad was such a good cook. Mom mainly made the biscuits for breakfast.

My parents always made sure all us kids were at the table and they could always tell if anybody was missing. After everybody was there Dad would always bless the food with a prayer of thanks to our Almighty God and then we would eat. We had to stand up at the table when we ate. Eventually Dad built benches for us kids to sit at the table and he built chairs for him and Mom.

Every year or so we would make sorghum syrup or what we called molasses. We had all the equipment to make it but since it was a major job to do Dad did not do it every year. He planted the cane and when it was ready in early Fall the boys would cut it down and haul it up to the mill. We would strip the leaves off.

I still have a scar on my left thumb from cutting myself with the cane. We had a horse to hitch up to the part where we fed the cane in to crush the juice out. Dad would build a fire under the pan that had several compartments. He would cook off one section and let it run out into milk cans. I always liked the foam that came up on top. I wasn't crazy about molasses but ate them with butter and biscuits if I had to. However, Mom did make molasses cookies. They were big and chewy. We took them to school in our lunches.

Chewing Gum

I would take my gum out of my mouth and stick it on my Grandparent's screen door and would go back to get it later. I was saving it while I ate those delicious cookies. It was like Christmas to see gum.

There were so many of us in the family and only five sticks of gum in a pack. So Dad would break the sticks in half to treat all us kids to the same pleasure of chewing this delightful treat. One day after my Dad returned from the store I asked him if he got us any half sticks of gum. He was amused by my question as he chuckled a bit.

Clothes on Our Back

We were very poor and usually only got one pair of shoes each year. Since there were so many of us we couldn't all fit into a car or truck and our parents probably couldn't afford to buy all of our shoes at once, we got around at different times to go to town and shop.

But most the time our parents would measure our feet toe to heel and order the shoes from the Sears Roebuck catalog services. We would send the drawings into Sears and in a few days the new shoes arrived. Hand me downs were rare with our shoes. We would go barefoot as soon as the snow melted.

Mom was a good seamstress and taught herself on the old treadle sewing machine. When Mom was outside the boys, especially Howard, liked to loosen the belt on the machine and see how fast they could work it.

Mom made her own sewing patterns and got real good making the boys overalls. She would make our dresses from cloth chicken feed sacks with pretty prints on them. In fact, when Dad would leave for town to stock up on feed and groceries, Mom would usually tell him to get two or three feed sacks with the same prints so she could finish making a dress.

CHAPTER THREE:
MY TEENAGE YEARS

I attended Conway high school but I had a watchdog, my brother Don, with his daily report to Dad. I made good grades in spite of it all. I made the girls volleyball team but couldn't play, didn't have transportation home from volleyball practices after school. So I would play at noontime or whenever I could during school hours. I was a good spiker. The coach was about seven feet tall. I would go against him and get it much of the time.

I was the top student in our commerce class, that was typing and writing shorthand. I could take down 120 words per minute in shorthand. However, I wasn't that good of a typist, slow but accurate. Anyway being the top student I got to go to a state contest in Jefferson City. That was in my eleventh year of school.

Jail House

I don't think I even got to go to town until I was about ten years old. I know Mom and Dad commented one day they didn't want us to see the liquor signs flashing. As it would be a bad influence on us. Evidently my brother Howard got loose and saw a lot of them flashing. I guess he was an alcoholic.

One day Howard raised the trunk of his car, low and behold there were several cases of beer in there. He taught all the younger brothers how to drink. Howard got put in jail quite a bit and Dad would always pay his fines to get him out. I think Dad finally got tired of spending his money so foolishly. Howard probably thought it was just all a game. He acted so irresponsibly.

All during high school my older brother Don would go home and tattle to my Dad about everything I did and who I rode to town with at noon. At this time Daddy preached at Little Vine Freewill Baptist Church and tried to keep a tight reign on us kids, especially the girls.

I was sixteen at the time and all the boys attended his church thinking he would eventually let me date one of them. Among the boys were two brothers Bill and Lester Jinks. I liked Lester real well and would sit between the two brothers during

during church service. It bothered my Dad so much that he wouldn't even take me to church there. I had to just stay home on the farm way out in the country.

The two brothers were older and out of school so they would drive to Conway a lot of the days and take me out to lunch. Sometimes they would wait in town and I would ride home with them. Naturally my brother Don kept Dad informed on every little detail and then I got preached to again.

And then there was a neat looking guy at Little Vine church. His name was Don Hicks. So he asked me if he could take me home from church one night. I took my chances of getting a belting from Dad and let Don drive me home. We went the back road so we would beat Dad home from church. Don had a station wagon and the backdoor squeaked. He said, "I think I'll get back there and put my foot in it." Don stopped somewhere and gave me a kiss and then more kisses.

He was a very likeable guy but I think he was afraid of my Dad. So he began dating another girl Lodeme Buttram and later on he married somebody I didn't know. However, sometime back Don asked one of my brothers about me.

Oh and I remember Glen Alford from Wright County who went to our church. He really tried to get to me so he decided to pick up his bible and head to church where he attempted to preach. He thought, "Well now if I do the preaching ritual, Andy will surely let her go out with me."

Wrong, Glen came into our house on a Sunday night with Bible in hand. He sat down and asked my Dad if he could take me to Church at Eureka that night. Dad just gave him that far off look and said no she can't go. Glen got up and left. I asked my Dad why I couldn't go with him. He said, "Cause his Grandpa stole jelly from someone's cellar years ago." I really think my Dad was afraid of Glen after that episode, as Glen had his heart set on me. He attended Church and just glared at Dad when he preached.

I was never allowed to date Glen, despite the fact that he was a well dressed, clean cut guy, didn't smoke or drink. At this point I was getting real upset with how my Dad intended to keep his thumb on me. I would have run away from home but didn't know where to go. It was about like being in jail.

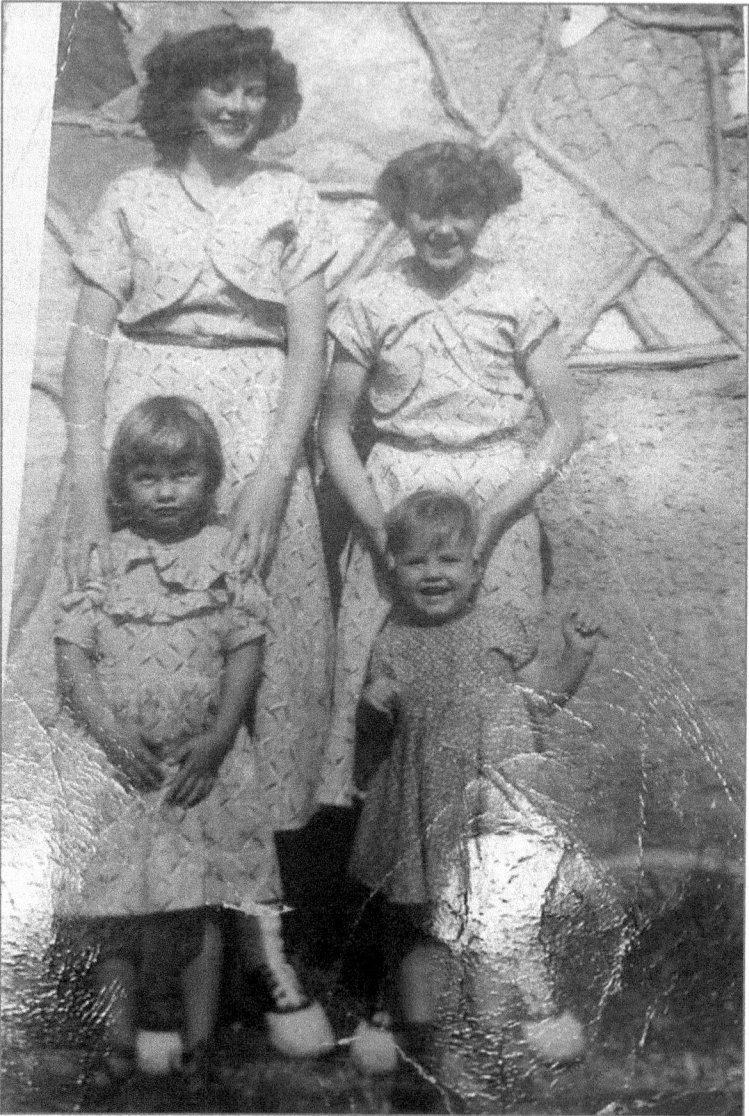

From back left: Leona and Grace and front left: Ann and Jean.

When I was in my eleventh year of school I was allowed
to go to the Junior Senior prom with my date, Frankie Baker, who

was already out of school. So we were going to get together and he was to bring me home from the prom. But low and behold when I got to the exit door at the school, there stood my Dad. I heard his words, "Lets go home." I did and was very unhappy.

It was all I could do to remain living at home and just work and go to school. I would of rather been behind bars. I would of had more freedom. One of our cousins Lucy came in from Michigan and saw what we all had to deal with. So she wanted me to come move in with her after high school. Lucy was planning to enroll me at a business college in Michigan. I don't recall my Dad saying I could go so I started trying to find a way of escape.

My sister Mary and her husband Harry, a Baptist preacher, knew of a fellow Baptist minister in the Licking, Missouri area. They both evidently knew Dad would never let me leave or even go with anyone if he wasn't a preacher. So the reverend Bob Copeland came down with them one day and I let him come back in about two weeks. He was a Southern Baptist Minister and also a schoolteacher.

Bob lived about a hundred miles away so we wrote each other in between him driving down to visit me. He had been through college and several years in the Air Force and had been teaching a few years. Bob said he was 26 years old. I thought he done a lot and crowded it in the time frame but I didn't question it at this point.

Bob was preaching at a church in Licking and also teaching at a school there. He got serious with me right away. My parents even let me go with him to see where he worked one Saturday. Of course, we were always back under Dad's roof so he could guard us after dark.

I was still in high school and doing a good job, but Bob said, "Come on and let's get married and you can finish school at Licking." We got married and after getting settled in with him Bob decided I didn't need to finish school. Apparently he thought there were too many big boys in my class. Anyways, Bob had two jobs and said he could make us a living so I didn't really need my high school diploma.

In 1944, Bob in the Air Force at St. Louis before he was shipped over to be part of the Battle of the Bulge during World War II.

Me and Bob back in the day.

CHAPTER FOUR:
PREACHER'S WIFE

We met the middle of December in 1955 and were married March 16, 1956. I should've picked up on Bob's possessiveness but I was mainly trying to get away from my Dad's strict rules. Now I began to realize I jumped out of the frying pan and into the fire.

I got real homesick after we were first married. I had never spent any time away from my parents. Bob took me home about every two or three weeks. I would just cry. Even though Dad was very strict with me I still missed them.

Not long after we were married I got pregnant. My Mom's half-sister, Hazel Dull, made the comment that I had to get married. But I set her straight and said, "Dear Hazel, I was a virgin when I married Bob. You can talk and believe what you want but I am the one who knows the truth. You can't always judge others by yourself."

Bob and I moved to Summersville not long after we were married, I think at the end of the school term. We were closer to a hospital located in Salem, Missouri and found a lady doctor there. Her name was Alice Crosby and she was a good doctor. She had four children of her own, including a pair of twins. Close to my delivery date I developed a kidney infection and had to be watched more closely.

Motherhood

Our first son was born in December of 1956. He weighed in at 9 pounds 1 ounce and was 23 inches long. We named him Robert Bruce Jr., but he has always been Bobby to me. I was so proud of him. The month of January was very gloomy so I would just lay on the bed with him while he slept.

We decided to move to Niangua, closer to my parents. Bob got a church and a school there so we lived in Kenneth Lee's old house. It was not a modern house. There were cabinets in the kitchen and one day I opened one up to get a dish and there lay a snake.

Leona and Bob with little Bobby.

Bobby was getting hard to keep up with so we bought a playpen. He wasn't about to stay in there so he figured out how to raise the bottom up and crawled out. One morning when Bobby was about 2 or so years old I got out early to hang out clothes. Our house was located along a gravel county road with pretty busy traffic.

I heard gravel crunching and I looked up. Our car was parked on an incline and Bobby was in it. He had shifted the gear out of park and rolled right across the road at risk of any oncoming traffic. The barbed wire fence caught the car before rolling further down the mountainous hillside.

Bobby had all the car doors locked. I ran as fast as I could down the hill and across the road without looking for traffic to our car to see he was ok. This whole thing scared Bobby as much as it did me. It took some effort to convince my baby boy to unlock the car door. I had to promise not to spank him so I could convince my baby boy to unlock the door for Mommy.

Another time not long after the car incident Bobby decided he would take his tricycle out on the road like the big cars do. But, he got a good spanking for that one. He always remembered there were no promises made with that adventure and he never tried it again.

Bob served at the First Baptist Church at Niangua and also the Good Spring Baptist Church while we lived in the area. The church members fixed Sunday dinner for us back then, which was very nice. We still live in the old house on Kenneth Lee's property. I had an uncle, Walt Barker, regularly mow our lawn. He was due to mow our lawn on one particular day and I had just finished my ironing.

I had a black dress and a black belt and as I was entering the front door I saw my belt laying on the bedroom floor. I thought I hung it up after I finished ironing. So as I stepped closer it moved. Low and behold a big black snake, right there in the corner of our bedroom.

I called out to Uncle Walt and he came on up and killed that thing. Gave off such a terrible odor, forcing me to open up all the doors and windows. By this time and after the earlier experience with the snake sunbathing in our kitchen cabinet, I was wanting to move. We had mice and anywhere a mouse can go a snake can go too.

I recall another funny incident with Bobby. Let me set the stage. As I stated earlier our house was not modern. We had a well where we drew up buckets of water from and a wash pan to wash in and a bucket with a dipper for drinking. Anyways we had a Sunday dinner at one of the parishioner's homes.

Right before dinner I told Bobby to go wash hands in the bathroom. I didn't hear any running water and the bathroom facilities were nearby where I would have heard. So when Bobby came back from the bathroom I asked him, "Son, I didn't hear the water running, are you sure you washed your hands?" He replied, "Mom, they already had it ready for me." Bobby had washed his hands in the potty. We all had a good laugh with that.

Bob and Bobby

I recall one time when Bobby was in a beginners Sunday school class. He was around five or so years old at the time. As soon as church was over for the day, his teacher Rose Huenefeld came up to me. She told me that she asked the students what bothered them the most with things that happened at home.

Each one took their turn answering. When it got to Bobby's turn he said, "You know its my Mom and Dad's bed, it squeaks a lot while I'm trying to sleep." Rose got such a kick out of that and couldn't wait to share it with me. We both had such a good laugh.

Life Challenges

Eventually we left that area and moved to Montevallo, Missouri, a small town near Nevada Missouri. I think Bob misjudged this move. We weren't there very long as I recall. He usually let the Lord lead, but it's amusing how more money seemed to make a lot of difference in our moving.

We didn't have a television as Bob didn't think we should have that junk funneled into our house. So we went to our neighbors and watched hers. Bob couldn't seem to get a school contract in the area. He substituted as a teacher but that wasn't enough to get by on.

We haven't lived there not even a year and we got up and moved to St. Charles, Missouri where two of his brothers Earl and Raymond lived. Bob got a teaching position at The Orchard Farms School and filled in at different churches in the area. One church stands out in particular to me. It was sort of a mission at Weldon Springs.

Riley and Eva Mead from St. Louis were the regular ministers at that church. They were an older couple and pretty much adopted us as their own. That seemed to be the real reason for moving to the St. Charles area. Sadly enough Riley had developed Muscular Dystrophy and not long thereafter suffered towards a terrible death.

My brother-in-law Earl was a building contractor and he moved us into one of his houses. It was the old thing they raised their four kids in. His wife Opal worked at the Bronn Shoe Company there and was such a filthy housekeeper. We now lived in the 4-bedroom house he and his sons built that needed a lot of repairs, pretty much a facelift.

They took their time fixing it up. We were eventually going to buy the house, but Bob really never wanted to buy and settle down. He always wanted to be ready to move if the Lord called him somewhere else. I never fully unpacked all boxes even at this early part of our marriage. I could tell Bob was going to be on the go.

Bob heard about a church at Raymondville, Missouri so we moved there. A couple, Wilmer and Marion Dietrich were main members in that church and her mother lived with them. They kept Bobby a lot when we had church meetings to attend or school activities to be at. Bob always taught school along with pastoring the smaller country or small-town churches.

We had to rent there and there wasn't much to choose from. We rented the lower section of a big two-story house. The lady who owned the house worked away during the week and only stayed at the house on the weekends. She sure was a bossy old heifer. The house was large but not modern. There was no indoor bathroom so we had a pot we used at night and threw the contents over a fence out back. The old lady got on us about that. The tissue made a mess.

We had something real weird happen there one night. A light like a candle appeared in our bedroom when we were in the bed talking. The light floated over to the window and went out. It was scary at first. Bob got up and grabbed his bible and read something out of it. I saw him reading the words but I just didn't hear him, maybe I was just too scared.

Anyways I believe Bob thought it was a sign to move on to Winona, Missouri. This time we lived in a nice parsonage next to our new church. It was nice and modern but the church members ran in and out like they owned it and actually they did. I always thought they built the parsonage close to the church so they could keep tabs on it.

I was pregnant again during this time and got so heavy. I gained fifty pounds each time I was pregnant. My back would hurt a lot then too. Bobby took up with Jean Weaver and her husband Pyrt. Bobby figured out a short cut to their house from our parsonage. On several occasions Jean would call and ask, "Are you missing something, Leona?" Being pregnant I just didn't feel like playing with Bobby like I should have so he would go to Jean for attention.

One time I saw smoke at the back of the church. In panic I ran fast as I could over there to find Bobby with a matchbox. He had built a fire at the back door of the church. All of the matches were on fire so I quickly got that put out before the church went up in smoke. Bobby was five years old at the time.

I dressed Bobby up in his little suits and bow ties. He was well behaved in church so we would let him sit on the front row during church services. Bobby loved sitting in front so he could watch the pianist play. After service was over Bobby would go up to the piano and start playing by ear what he heard the pianist previously played in the church service.

So Pyrt was the song leader and when the regular pianist was absent he would get Bobby on the piano and we would have music. Being short as a five-year old would be, Bobby's feet couldn't even reach the piano pedals. Despite that we got through the church service and he got so he could play real good and even threw in all his extra notes. We saw we had a child prodigy on our hands that we were going to have to deal with the best we could.

Baby Brother

It was time for our new baby to arrive. I had Dr. T.J. Burns in Texas county at Houston, Missouri. Labor pains early of the morning with both boys. Dr. Burns first words were, "I bet this boy weighs ten pounds." A few minutes later the doctor came in to check on me and I asked him, "How much did he weigh?" And he replied, "Nine pounds seven ounces." I forgot to mention that Dr. Burns was one of our former president's doctors to Harry S. Truman. I had indeed been in good hands with him.

We chose a Bible name of Phillip and his middle name of Eugene, named after one of Bob's nephews, Eugene Copeland. We just thought the two names went well together. So we now had Phillip Eugene Copeland born in August of 1962.

Bobby was so proud to have a little brother to play with. The age difference could be a problem. There was five year nine months between the boys. I wanted them closer to each other in age but I miscarried about three years before this.

Bobby ran a lot of errands, such as bringing a fresh diaper or baby bottle. One day everything was just too quiet so I went in to check on the new baby. To my surprise Bobby was trying to change his baby brother's diaper. Scared me real good as he could have stuck the little guy with one of those big diaper pins. Bobby had the diaper pin open and was trying to get it done. He could of

probably accomplished what he sat out to do but I did draw the line that day.

When Phillip was only a few weeks old, Bob and I weren't thinking and we left somewhere in the car and a few blocks down the road I said, "Oh we forgot the baby." So Bob turned the car around and we went back for him.

Phillip was anemic at birth. I took all the vitamins the doctor told me to take but he was still short on iron. So we had to start him on iron drops immediately. Phillip had asthma attacks a little bit later on and was very unhealthy. Seems as if we had him on antibiotics most of the time. He had a lot of ear, nose, and throat problems.

Phillip wouldn't talk for a long time. He would point and grunt and we would answer to that. He didn't walk very early either and cut his first tooth at ten months old. He wasn't nearly as hard to raise as Bobby was. Bobby was the busy one. Phillip was laid back and didn't care what went on.

Phillip had a lot of artistic abilities. He would sit and draw some of the scariest looking cartoon characters at such an early age. So again we think we have another gifted son.

On the Move Again

Yet again it was time to move. We left our things at the parsonage in Winona and ended up renting a mobile home at Hillsboro, Missouri. I thought I would find a parttime job and help out with the expenses. I got word that a local construction company needed a secretary so I went to apply and got the job. The superintendent was a really good looking dude and naturally with Bob being so possessive I should of known better than try being a private secretary. Bob called him up and said I wouldn't be there. I was scheduled to report to work the next day.

There was fifteen years between Bob and me. He treated me same as one of his school pupils, like I was his little girl to raise. That was getting old at this point and I knew I'd made a big mistake but tried to make the best of it as there were two little boys to raise. I was determined to make a happy home for them. It was so hard to do and as a minister's wife the church people expected us all to be angels.

Bob (top middle) at his graduation to receive his PhD. He was now Dr. Robert B. Copeland.

They also expected me to be able to play the piano and teach a Sunday School class. I took piano lessons and played in one recital. After that I decided the churches weren't going to decide what I was to do in order to be the perfect minister's wife. Playing the piano wasn't easy for me so I gave that idea up.

Things didn't work out for us at Hillsboro so we moved to Couch, Missouri. Bob preached at Riverton Baptist Church. We rented a nice house there but the owners decided to sell it so we found a house farther from the church but still in Couch. We had some good neighbors there, Price and Mabel Frey.

They had no children and immediately took up with our two boys. Price and Mabel would keep Phillip when we had to go out at night. Mabel was so good with our little Phil. They looked us up later on in life and said they missed Phillip so much. He has a purple and blue quilt she made for him. Just very nice people. Ralph and Mary Combs were more good neighbors. Ralph was our mail carrier.

Bob, Leona, Bobby, and Phillip in front of our house.

We had a few chickens at this house. I went out one day to gather the eggs and a black snake was in the chicken nest devouring the eggs. I let him have them all and went back about my business to the house. I sure seem to have some bad luck running into snakes from childhood to adulthood.

After living at Couch for awhile we yet again packed up our stuff and moved to Big Springs, Missouri, north of Herman. Bob was the principal at the elementary school there and was also a pastor at a Baptist Church in the same town. That was a big mistake having the two jobs that close with the same kids involved in both the same school and the same church.

The custodian position opened up so Bob thought I could do that since he would know where I was and that I would not be around other guys. I did the clean up after school. Bob was also the junior high school coach which included volleyball which I knew more about that sport than he did. Shoot I could still play as good as when I was in high school.

Any who, Bob asked the school superintendent if I could coach the girls volleyball team and he said ok. So I got to go to all of the games and used my own judgement and did a good job with them. Everybody was impressed and the girls liked my style.

Bobby was seven years old at this time. We bought a piano and started him on lessons. His first piano teacher was Marjorie Green at Herman, Missouri. She was intrigued by his natural ability to play everything by ear or as he heard it. Bobby took lessons from her as long as we lived in Big Springs.

Bobby tried to follow her instruction but he tended to throw in those extra notes at times. She taught him well and at the young age of ten he played for a big church wedding. The wedding was for Diane Moore, one of our church members and also one of Bob's school students.

Bobby had all his music together for the wedding and enough for a normal circumstance. But, the groom was running late and I knew my son was worried while he was playing and looked back at me. So I passed a note up to him by the usher and told him to start his music all over and then just begin playing the March soon as the whole party got there.

He did a fine job and was real confident about it. One thing I do regret is Bobby never got to be a little boy. He had to grow up too fast He was in everything at school where music was involved.

I thought maybe I could get Bob interested in buying us a house in Big Springs area instead of renting one. So Kenneth Gerloff had his up for sale. It wasn't very old and a nice three bedroom ranch with a two car garage. We applied for a VA loan. All the paperwork went through except they said the well casing needed to be somewhat higher up.

Unfortunately, we would have to pay the expense to get it fixed. Bob wouldn't get it fixed so I didn't get my house I wanted so bad. I don't think Bob wanted to settle down yet. Guess it was probably about time for me to start packing for another move. I was so disappointed.

While we were in Big Spring my brother J.D. and his wife Leona came to visit us. Their daughter Debbie and Phillip were about six weeks apart in age. They looked so cute outside playing together. I have some pictures from that.

We had some good people in the church in Big Springs, but we also had Ralph Uthlaut, a state representative and they were our neighbor and we thought our friends. However, they weren't members of our church, but they had two boys there at the school.

One of them could play ball and the other one couldn't. So in his role as a basketball coach at the school Bob would play the representative's older boy but let the younger one sit on the bench. Ralph and Bob butted heads. The representative attended all of the games both home and away, constantly calling Bob out on several things about the game.

He eventually saw that Bob was not going to give into him so Ralph schemed to get him fired. The politician got his mission accomplished. Ralph had stated that Bob got too preachy in the classroom and held prayer at noon. Those were his main complaints. So the school superintendent offered Bob a transfer to the school in Herman, Missouri but we thought it was too degrading to stay there and look across the road every day at them. So we made plans to move once again.

Family Struggles

One day back in the 1960's, I got a phone call from my Aunt Flossie, my Dad's only sister. I don't know why she chose to call me. I wasn't the oldest or closest in distance from my parents. Maybe she knew I would be there and get something done.

Anyway, my Dad was in the hospital in Lebanon, Missouri. Why in the world would they ever take him there. It wasn't even what I would classify a good veterinary clinic. I got there as soon as I could. He had been there three or four days and very sick. Dad was beginning to turn yellow.

First thing Dad said was he had gall stones and they were scheduling him for surgery the next day. I told him I need his permission first and I was going to transfer him to the hospital in Springfield, Missouri where he would have a better chance of living through it. The folks at Lebanon hospital about convince him to get the surgery done there but finally he consented to be moved.

Dad was so sick and in so much pain that he was now in the "I don't care" stage. A stone was blocking the bile duct and gave him Jaundice. The main doctor happened to be at the nurse's station So I introduced myself to him and told him I was moving him to Springfield. He quickly responded, "Oh no, you can't. We're going to operate on him at 1:00 p.m. tomorrow."

I was very young around 22 or 23 years old but quite aggressive so I didn't take his response very well. I stared right dead into his eyes and stated to this man, "Doctor, all I need to know is if my Dad can ride in my car or do I need an ambulance. This is my Dad and I intend to do what I feel best for my Dad. He has been here three or four days and you all haven't even bothered to shave him so I can't believe you know what is even wrong with my Dad."

I asked the front desk how much was Dad's bill and they said $33. But when Dad received the bill in the mail later it was

$66. Those vindictive folks doubled the bill. I wouldn't have paid it and I don't know if Dad did or not.

Leona, Grace, and Pauline back in the day.

Anyways, Bob and I got Dad into the back seat of our car. He was in so much pain. I rode in the back and held a cold washcloth on his head while Bob broke the speed limit to get to Springfield. We arrived at Cox Medical Center in Springfield and got a surgeon lined up immediately.

Dad was so skeptical of the surgeon's knife so the doctor had to draw a picture of exactly the procedure he was going to take. They operated at one o'clock that night. It definitely was an emergency, the poison was going to kill my Dad. They took out 29 stones and the rotten gall bladder. Dad was very sick for several days after the surgery and gradually recovered enough to leave after being there for a total of nineteen days.

Leona with her sisters while visiting at Mom and Dad's house back on the farm.

Then about two weeks after this whole ordeal with my Dad, I developed a high fever that skyrocketed to 105 degrees. I was at Mom and Dad's when I got real sick. So I was admitted to the hospital in Salem, Missouri. Test after test after test done and the doctors just couldn't figure out what was wrong with me. Finally I started turning yellow, the white part of my eyes and even my stomach. They diagnosed me with infectious hepatitis. I suppose I picked up the germ from Dad having the Jaundice caused by the Gall stones.

I stayed in the hospital for two weeks. It was a hot summer and there was no air or not even a fan in my room so it made for a pretty miserable stay. I thought I was going to die so I checked myself out of the hospital and went home. I couldn't lift anything because my liver was in bad shape so they said.

Several family members had the hepatitis, all who were around me when my high fever struck. I remember Jack's wife Carol had it. She about died as the doctors were treating her for something else.

During the time we live in Big Springs, I got tired of cleaning at the school so I applied for a job at the Hawthorne Company at New Haven, Missouri. This is where one of my younger brothers comes into the picture. Perry was a good kid but at the age of 21 he got to drinking and ended up in some serious trouble with the law in Webster County.

The court wouldn't let Perry go back home as Dad couldn't control him. They were going to send him to the state penitentiary at Jefferson City, Missouri. So they called me to see if Bob and I would take responsibility for Perry. That was such a hard decision to make since we were raising two little boys. I really wondered what I should do. I was torn between helping my younger brother and exposing my boys to this whole mess with the thought in the back of mind if we would even be able to control Perry's actions while he lived with us.

I reckon I couldn't stand to see him sent up to the big house, so I travelled to the courthouse in Marshfield, Missouri to get him paroled to me. Perry had a parole officer assigned over him. He had to report to the officer I believe each month.

Perry got a good job at the Hawthorne Company, working as a head cutter. They made military tents there. I remember when I went to go work there before Phillip was in the first grade. My baby boy was so unhappy with the babysitter, who was one of our church members. I didn't work very long. Phillip got so he would cry when Bob took him there so we decided there was a problem. It was not until later when we learned that the babysitter was not very nice and would make my little boy go lay in the bed where their children had peed in it. They seemed like such good people but you can't judge a book by its cover.

Phillip was very unhealthy yet as a child. He had a cold about all of the time and struggled through often serious asthma attacks. On occasion we had to rush him late night to the Dr. J.R. Knudsen in Herman, Missouri. His little heart would beat so fast during his asthma attacks.

In such desperate emergencies the doctor was forced to give Phillip very risky shots, but they always worked. After they would give him a shot we would have to wait at the doctor's office for about an hour. The doctor would observe Phillip's condition until he was breathing normal again. My baby boy always came through with his strong spirit in his little body.

Anyways, back to Perry coming to live with us in Big Springs, Missouri. We had three bedrooms and bunk beds for the boys in one bedroom so no problem there. We had the third bedroom for Perry. When Perry moved in with us he weighed 160 pounds and when he left he weighed 190 pounds. He definitely didn't starve under our roof.

While living with us he had to attend our church. Actually, he met a girl there who was a member of the church. Her name was Verda Horn. They seemed to be hitting it off pretty good. However, I did continue to see a problem with Perry and his drinking. Perry and Verda eventually decided to get married.

I had a good deal of problems with Perry drinking. I now knew he was an alcoholic who needed more help than I knew how to give him. I just know all I could do was give him a home and cook for him while he stayed with us. By Perry getting married that automatically eliminated the parole officer assigned who tried to control his drinking.

Perry and Verda moved into an apartment in New Haven, Missouri and lived there awhile and then their baby girl, Lisa, was born. At this point they bought a nice mobile home and seemed to be doing okay. They frequently came to visit us and attend our church. They would also occasionally drive down to visit Mom and Dad. Verda's parents didn't live far from New Haven so Perry and Verda would visit them quite often as well. So they always saw family.

This photo of Perry was taken not too long before his death.

About a year or so had passed and their second daughter, Delores, was born. They didn't have anyone to keep their daughter Lisa while they were busy with the birth of Delores. So Bob and I decided we could do that job for them. When Bob would get ready for work, Lisa would hurry over with her walker and get her coat. She wanted to go along with Bob.

Evidently Lisa had a bad habit sleeping with Verda and Perry instead of in her own bed. She would not sleep in the bed we put up for her, constantly crying. So we would let her fall asleep in our bed and try transferring her but she would wake up instantly. She would sleep with her head on me and her feet touching Bob.

That was a terrible habit they started to let her sleep in their bed that needed to be broken. Fortunately, it only lasted a few days when Verda and Perry were now back home with the new baby. They came to pick up Lisa. Ah yes, all was normal again.

Perry liked to hunt wildlife as Dad always taught the boys how to shoot a gun. When Dad thought they were old enough he would load a gun and send one out alone. He told them to bring back a squirrel or rabbit. That was the way Dad taught the boys to hunt.

I had to go to Herman October 22, 1971 to take Bobby to his piano lesson. I met Perry as I was going in, little did I know that would be the last time I would see him alive. A call came in early Sunday morning, October 23rd. I answered and it was Verda. She wouldn't tell me anything, she asked for Bob. Then I realized by his conversation that Perry was dead.

Perry was killed in a one-car wreck near Big Springs, Missouri. He was only 27 years old and had left behind a widow with two daughters, 2 and 3 years old. The callous thing about this was how the highway patrol notified Verda by phone instead of visiting her at home to convey the bad news with any sort of condolences and to offer any help if she needed it.

If I remember right there may have been alcohol involved. I went to the scene of the accident after they picked up my brother's body. The motor had flipped out of his 1962 Chevrolet car and fell on top of him, crushing his chest.

We held a funeral service for Perry at Herman. Then we took the body back to Eureka for burial. I believe my brother J.D. was the one who called Mom and Dad with the bad news. At this time my Dad was terminally ill with lung cancer and couldn't leave his bed at home near Eureka. So before burying Perry at

Eureka graveyard, we had arranged for the funeral director to bring Perry's casket to my parent's house. Dad had to see to know his son was really gone.

Looking back before this tragedy took place, Dad had been fighting cancer for about three years. He had pneumonia and they ex-rayed his lings and spotted a tumor. The doctors took the one lung out, it was completely full of cancer. I sat with him the night after his lung operation.

Dr. Polk was over his cancer problem. We took turns going down to take Dad for his checkups. I recall a time taking Dad for a checkup at Smith Glynn – Callaway Clinic and naturally you wait your turn regardless of how sick you are. I knew Dad looked bad and he made the statement, "I'd like to lay down here on the floor."

My youngest sister Jean posing for the camera and in the background is Dad standing out on the front.

He had lost so much weight a rib came through his side and had to have it sawed off. Then he got staph infection and could not get it cleared up so they put him in Mount Vernon which was really a J.B. Sanitarium, like a nut house for the crazies.

We had to put on gloves and gowns when we visited Dad. They had him in isolation. He was in the hospital for a hundred days in one year's time. Us girls helped Mom out a week at a time. She was breaking under the heavy load. It is so hard on the caregiver when there's a lingering or terminal sickness to deal with.

Mom holding her purse out in front of the house. Ann and Jean are standing on the porch.

So with all that already happening with Dad, it was very hard on both my parents when Perry was killed. I remember my Dad was so devastated as he struggled to pick up his now feeble body out of the bed, scooted a few steps over to the casket and grieved over the loss of his boy. This was such a very hard moment for all of us.

Seeing my Dad in such a fragile state leaning over the casket he said to Perry's body, "Perry it won't be long, I will be with you." Just about three months later Dad passed away January 18 of the following year.

Not long after Perry's funeral, his widow Verda moved to Omaha Nebraska with her two little girls and lived there ever since. She collected social security to help raise her daughters. She had a good job and was very independent, never asking for anything. I always thought she had such beautiful red hair. That is why I color mine auburn as I thought hers was such a pretty color. Verda eventually remarried to a good guy.

Then comes to mind my younger brother Glenn. He was dating Sharon Crum. She was a very attractive blonde, I think from California. They got married and had a son named Rex. They soon split up in divorce. She moved back to California with their kid. Glenn would go to California to snatch up the kid and head back to Missouri with him.

She would come to Missouri to do the same thing, taking him back to California. These two so called grownups would play this game several times. I never really knew which parent had custody of their son. I suppose Sharon did.

Then Glenn got remarried that also ended up in divorce. He married his third wife and that was another bad choice, yet another divorce. He luckily still only had the one son Rex. It didn't seem wise for Glenn to have custody of any kids who he would be stringing along all across the country.

Glenn and another of my younger brothers Wayne still had some wild oats to sow in the taverns. One night I got a call from some family member that Glenn had been shot in the leg. They had him in surgery and couldn't get the bleeding stopped. He and Wayne were somewhere at a tavern and Wayne supposedly had a pistol. I don't have enough exact details to elaborate on this incident.

Here is Glenn out back on the farm with a horse, barn is in the background.

Then awhile thereafter when Glenn was back to his normal life again he met Bonnie. She had two sons from a previous marriage. They got married and had a son named Landon. They all moved into the house that Glenn already owned in Lebanon. He also already had a good job close to home. Everything seemed good now with Glenn.

I hesitate to even mention my youngest brother Robert but this is probably the only time I do. The disdain between us was obvious. I did not pretend to hide my feelings at all. Well, sometime after my Dad's passing, my Mom had developed some heart problems but stayed on the farm anyways. When Robert married a local girl named Virginia, Mom decided to buy a trailer and set it near her house. The idea was for Robert and Virginia to move into the trailer and take care of Mom and the farm.

Seemed like if something wasn't free for Robert he would just take it from Mom. He didn't help out like he was supposed to do. All of us older children got together and bought Mom a new washer and dryer and we also put tile down on all the floors in her house. My youngest sisters Ann and Jean were the main children who cared for our Mother after Dad's death.

Robert had grown real impatient with our Mom. He was such a useless human being. I truly detested him and whenever I saw Robert I would never hesitate to call him out on his behavior. There was no sibling love. His only employment was a job playing in a rock band. He had let his hair grow long, resembling a hippy.

Rumor had it that he was implicated in some questionable things. Most involved drugs or violent behavior. At one point he had walked up to Mom's house from his trailer threw a knife in front of her and it stuck into her kitchen cabinet. She told me this herself. He was trying to scare her into moving out of the house so he would then have full control of the farm.

Mom had set a price of $20,000 for the 160 acres of farmland if Robert wanted to buy it. But he had another deal in mind. Robert would get Mom to sign over the property deed with no money down nor a contractual agreement in place and then kick her out of her house. He got his mission accomplished. Robert never paid her a red cent and as of 1995 he never tried to make amends to all the brothers and sisters involved and probably never intended to do such a thing. It would have been out of his horrible character.

So our Mom moved into the senior citizens housing at Marshfield, Missouri for a very low rent. Robert and Virginia moved into what used to be Mom's house. Mom sold the trailer she had bought and paid for and Robert wanted half the money and he got it. He was now back there on our family farm milking cows and letting everything on the farm run down. We speculated he would eventually lose the farm, sold at the courthouse door.

Karma eventually came back on Robert for all his bad deeds. He paid dearly for the farm. In 1999, his 19-year old son

Jesse was burned up in a truck accident. There were traces of three or four different drugs involved according to the coroner's report. Most of the family was in denial about the drugs. Jesse learned everything about drugs from his Dad. Sometimes the price for sin can be very high.

Back to my brother Wayne. I always thought he got a lot of spankings that Robert should have had. Wayne served in the Navy. He bought 40 acres of land in Wright County from Dad. When Wayne went away he had papers drawn up so if something should happened to him I could pay off the 40 acres and it would be mine.

Wayne had a lot of resentment towards Dad. I tried to be good to my brother. Wayne and I had several yard sales together. He lived in Springfield when I lived in Marshfield so he would stop by McDonald's and bring out our breakfast, then I had food made for lunch. I would always ask Wayne if he stopped drinking. He would always say, "I have it under control. I can drink or not drink." He picked some blackberries and I made him several jars of jelly one year.

Wayne was very intelligent and had some college hours under his belt. He worked for FEMA and was also in the real estate business. He would buy 100 acres and sell it in 10-acre plots. Wayne was always finding ways to make the money.

Then one day I received a phone call from his oldest daughter Casey. She told me he was in the veteran's hospital in Columbia, Missouri on life support. So I drove up to see him and when I walked into his room I said to him, "You sure had it under control." His liver and lungs were gone and he was swollen all over.

One of his doctors came into the room while I was there and he said, "If it is any consolation to you, we have him heavily sedated, he is feeling no pain." I thanked him for what he said. Wayne lived ten days after that day. That was my third alcoholic brother to die. Their bodies are all buried in the Eureka cemetery where Mom and Dad are buried.

Here is a pic of me with my Grandson Phil This is a good place to put something that makes me happy after talking about my brother Wayne passing away like he did.

CHAPTER FIVE:
SETTLING DOWN FOR AWHILE

We never seemed to stay much more than a year anywhere we lived. And yet again we were about to leave Big Springs thanks to the state representative who got Bob fired. So Bob was checking out churches and teaching employment around Missouri. He came up with a good school position at Vandalia, a few hours away.

Bob started as a sixth grade teacher there. He usually taught the higher level grades and was also acting in the role as the principal much of the time. Bob was stern teacher but didn't assign a lot of homework to his students. He always said if the teacher was doing their job thoroughly there wouldn't be a lot of homework. Parents caught word of his reputation and would always request for him as the teacher for their kids.

As Bob always seems to do, he also found an available church in need of a preacher located in Bowling Green which was about 17 miles east of Vandalia. The Immanuel Church had recently split off from the main Baptist Church and was rather small in membership. He was faced with a lot of work to increase the number of members.

I insisted we move somewhere and settle down so the boys can complete their schooling. All the moving around was just not good for them. Since our new church was small they didn't offer a parsonage. So we had to look around for a house to rent. A couple who were members of our church, Junior and Lucy Burris, had an older house so we moved into there.

Church Stuff and a Little Drama

I was asked to take the G.A. Leaders position at the church. That was an organization in the Southern Baptist Convention for younger girls. We would hold weekly meetings at our house every Friday after school. The members would all come over on the school bus and I would take them all home after our meetings were over.

As with all of our previous churches I also taught Sunday school here as well. I also attended all of the W.M.S. meetings and usually held an officer's position. Matter of fact, when we were in the Bear Creek Association, I had the B.J.U. director's job for the whole county of churches. I held numerous meetings and did it all.

One of our church members was John Warner, a bachelor who lived with his mother. He tried to date one of my younger sisters Ann who he had only heard about through me but never met her. Well, one day he made a goofy remark that he didn't see how she could be as pretty as I was. Such a nut. I think he was trying to flirt with me and I wouldn't have any of that. Such a jerk.

Taking Care of my Boys

Things were getting busy with my sons. Phillip was now starting first grade. His teacher was Ms. Motley. She was an old witch. Phillip didn't like her at all. We had several pretty intense confrontations with her which involved the principal. Somehow we survived the school year with her. I heard later on that she was so mean to all of her students. I think she needed Jesus or maybe a good paddling from the principal. The latter would have been fine with me.

Phillip had the opposite experience with his teacher in the second grade. Mrs. Willis was a real good teacher. She was an older black lady who would give all of her students hugs and really acted like she enjoyed teaching. Such a wonderful change from his previous teacher, that evil heifer Ms. Motley.

Phillip had joined a Cub Scout troop where he met his new buddy Ralph Atkinson. Them and a bunch of their troop buddies would camp out in Ralph's family travel trailer. They always had such a good time, scaring themselves by telling scary campfire stories.

Ralph's Father taught at the high school there. He also drove a school bus and was a driver's ed instructor. Ralph's Mother worked at one of the banks. They were a very nice and happy family. So we felt we could trust Phillip to stay over night at their house on occasion.

Joe Miller was another one of Phillip's buddies. His Mother was single and raised his whole family of like 6 kids I think. She was a hard working lady and I applaud her for raising such a fine boy like Joe. And Bobby also knew Joe's sister Diana who was Bobby's age.

Bobby and Phil standing in front of our church.

We had to find Bobby a new piano teacher. There was one we heard of, Mrs. Mitchell. She was a wife of the Presbyterian Minister there in Bowling Green. So we got Bobby all set up again with lessons. She was an older lady and taught him as long as she could but Bobby was just too advanced to learn anything more from her.

That was when we had to start taking him to a college music professor in Columbia, Missouri. That was about an hour or so round trip each week. Bobby was an advanced student even at this level of instruction by the college professor.

Bobby had a perfect ear pitch so any time folks had an acapella number at school or a contest, they used him. He had also taught himself to play the organ and even had his own piano students to teach. Things looked good for Bobby. He played for our church and special events around the entire area spanning several counties. I remember he played quite a few events out at a large Catholic church in St. Clements, Missouri.

While Bobby was in high school he played the trumpet and French horn in the band. I attended a lot of his activities. Us parents had the band boosters club that helped raise extra money for the band. I was elected secretary of the club one year and the next year I was elected president. I reckon they liked how I rolled.

When Bobby was in his third year of high school he and three friends decided to start up a Christian music group, calling themselves the Ambassadors for Christ. Bobby was the group leader, then there was Kevin Fryrear, Ron Tinsley, and Marion Branstetter. They bought all of their equipment and travelled around the region for musical engagements.

Their group was getting pretty popular and even ended up hosting the Lester Family group at an event at the Bowling Green high school. The Lester Family was from St. Louis and had their own weekly television show. So this was pretty big stuff and the boy's concert at the high school had a big turnout in attendance. The Ambassadors of Christ cut I think three music albums while they were together singing. However, the group broke up after high school. All of the boys had gone off to different colleges. Bobby got a full four-year music scholarship at the George Washington University in St. Louis, Missouri.

Some of My Friends

We met Mary Williams at the time we bought Bobby a new lawnmower so he could earn some money. She was his first customer. Mary became such a dear friend and second mother to me. Mary was born October 5, 1900, such a classy act. During her working years she was county assessor for Pike County, Missouri. She was a dressy lady, always wore a hat. When the boys started their music group Mary Williams and another one of my friends Martha Green were always there wherever the boys sang.

Mary was in the hospital several times during the time I knew her. I remember one time she had an emergency Gall stone operation and was so very sick. Not too long after Mary decided to move from her big white two-story house into Senior housing out in St. Clements, about 7 miles from her house Bowling Green.

I would come by to visit her and take her out to eat. Mary was a member of the Christian Church in Bowling Green. She was a real inspiration to me during the years I knew her. I just enjoyed being with her. She shared a lot of words of wisdom. Being a widow for 45 to 50 years, Mary showed me one can survive alone in this world. She only had two grandsons.

Ultimately Mary had to be put in a nursing home. The truly sad part about this, about ten years earlier her only daughter had died at the age of sixty. She apparently had something wrong with her heart that was irreparable. When Mary moved she gave me her beautiful china cabinet and an assortment of beautiful plates and other dishes. Not too long after she passed away in the Fall of 1994. We attended her funeral service at the chapel in Bowling Green.

Some other friends, Jack and Joann Floyd, lived a couple blocks down the street from our house. Jack was the Chief of Police in Bowling Green. Joann was the dispatcher for the police and fire departments.

I took on the dispatcher job part time and had radios and phones installed in our house. I had a regular phone to catch the police department calls, one all the fire calls came in on and I had a dispatch phone. I would just raise up the receiver on the dispatch phone and it had ten or twelve firemen's numbers that automatically dialed. I just had to tell them a few times where the fire was. Then the radio I talked on to the police cars, the sheriff or anyone else needing something. It was an interesting job. The pay wasn't that great but I was able to work from home.

Jack and Joann liked to party and they also drank a lot, especially Jack. It was told he could put away a 12 pack of beer every night. They had a son Jack Jr. who was maybe a couple of years older than Phillip. They always played together with the other neighborhood kids.

Bob thought I was in good hands when went with Joann to Hannibal, Missouri. But she was one wild woman. Joann ran around on Jack quite frequently. I think his drinking problem ruined their sex life so she went elsewhere for that.

Then there was another family we associated with, Bill and Dorothy. He was about twenty years older than her. They had three sons. They had a farm mainly raising pigs and Bill also had a pretty big car dealership in Bowling Green.

I remember I would run out to their farm on occasion to check out the old sows and see if they were pigging. They had us over for several good meals, some of those pigs sure were tasty. When we wanted to return the favor we would always take them out to eat. We didn't have a fancy house and not much dining area.

Their oldest son Mike went into the National Guard. I think he was trying to avoid the draft. But anyway Dorothy wanted him home and came to Bob for help as a minister to draw up hardship papers to bring her son home. Bob got the job done, he knew what he was doing since he was in the Air Force. Not sure I mentioned it but Bob actually was in the Battle of the Bulge during World War II. He never talked about it though so I never asked about it.

Mike ended up living in North Carolina. I recall he had caught pneumonia and was not doing well. So Dorothy and Bill decided they better go see about him. They took a ton of medicine to him and got him well.

Dorothy was a straight-laced person, but she liked her whiskey highballs during the day. She would offer me one but I never drank any. Their other sons were Robert and Eddie. The younger one ran with Dorothy too much and acted like a sissy. That was about all she had to hang onto as Bill and her were not close. I always wondered how they got those three boys.

Dorothy always thought Bill was having an affair with his secretary Myoma at his business. Dorothy treated him pretty cool, cooked for him and kept the house clean, but no more sex. He was much older than her and there was lots of money involved so Dorothy was not about to leave or divorce Bill.

Staying Busy with Work

While I kept busy with all of the church and school activities I also had several jobs during our stay in Bowling Green. I took on a job at Reaban's Restaurant. It was sort of a fast food place. Bob Beard was the owner. After working there awhile one night the place burned down. So that ended my employment there.

For three years I drove a school bus for the district. That was a pretty hard job. My bus route had over 70 kids, of which 20 of them were big boys in high school. There was John Cluster. I never will forget his name as I had him in the high school principal's office more than any other student on my bus.

One afternoon I was just driving along with a load bus of 70 kids and I saw John get up and then another boy who was 6 foot tall and probably weighed over 200 pounds. I saw John draw back to hit him so I did some quick thinking and hit my brakes. They both tumbled to the floor. When I stopped I threw on my flashers, got up out of the driver's seat and informed them in my kind way that I would be meeting them at Principal George Ninheuser's office the following morning.

I told the boys to get in their seats and stay there if they wanted to go home. I had to be stern or they would have overpowered me. I gave them ten days off my bus and the principal backed me up. George knew he better, I meant business.

Later in the Winter a big snow fell before school let out. Before I saw what happened one of the students opened a window, reached up and made a snowball. They evidently threw it at me, but splattered on my mirror. So I stopped the bus again and tried to find out which one did it.

I had a little girl in Junior High who kept an eye out for me. She was my informant on all that went on in the back of the bus. No one ever knew she called me at night to tell me everything I needed to know. If I could remember her name I would still try to find her and thank her for helping me.

Then there were two or three boys who decided they were going to cut one of the bus seats. I nailed them that day and got their names. I gave them to the principal who called these bad seeds into his office to decide on the punishment. Along with their punishment, their parents had to pay the cost of repairs for the damage done to the seats.

I remember an incident when a motorcycle ran past my bus when I had stopped with the stop light out to let the kids off the bus. Fortunately, the children getting off the bus had to cross the highway so they were safe.

Over the few years of driving the bus became increasingly stressful and I began having migraine headaches from the pressure. It got so bad that two or three times I had to radio in from the bus located somewhere along my bus route for them to send someone out for me and the bus. The migraines would start with blurred vision and ending in terrible headaches and nausea or vomiting. I finally gave up the bus diving job.

I took up a job as main cook in at the Maple Grove nursing home in Louisiana, Missouri, about ten miles away from Bowling Green. I worked from 6 in the morning until 2 in the afternoon. I liked my job, anything to do with cooking I really enjoyed.

Back in 1994 when I went to visit my past friend Mary Williams at the nursing home in Bowling Green I thought I had recognized a lady across the hall at my new job. So I went up and asked her and sure enough it was the same lady, Beulah O'Keefe.

I found out that she was another cook working there with me. She had a pretty rough life and her vocabulary was limited. One day something was said about our main boss Lewis Clough and Beulah said, "Shoot you don't know whether to shit or go blind," We all got a good laugh.

Bob's Siblings

Bob's brother Lee was married to a lady named Opal and had a son Les. Then not long after Opal divorced Lee and married his brother Earl. Between them they had two more sons Ed and John and then a daughter Pauline. All of the boys would help out Earl with his construction company. Bob always thought that Les belonged to Earl and Ed belonged to Lee. The physical make ups for each son would almost prove that. Pauline came and spent some time with us almost every summer.

When Pauline was all grown up I remember I went to my doctor's appointment at the hospital in Lake St. Louis and low and behold I accidentally ran into Pauline in the hallway. Apparently, she had a job working at the hospital so every time I went to my doctor's appointment I would have lunch with her. Pauline was such a delight. She had married Carol Stokes who had previously been married and they had two children.

Lee ended up having a stroke probably caused by all his drinking. He suffered a lot from paralysis from the stroke. He was sort of jumping around staying with all of the brothers. During the time we lived in Bowling Green it come our turn to take care of Lee.

An older brother Lewis and his wife Margaret lived in the Kansas City, Missouri area. They had three children: June, Jerry, and Eugene. The boys ended up helping their Dad in his construction business. All of the boys lived in Chillicothe, Missouri. Eugene was married but eventually divorced. The other two Jerry and June seemed to be happily married.

Years later when their company were building condos in Florida Jerry was on his way down there from Missouri when he had a terrible car accident. Jerry had died a short time after this tragedy.

I remember when Lewis's children were still kids living at home we went there one time to visit them when we were in the area for a teacher's convention. Then later on they came to visit us but their reason was to bring Lee to stay with us. They thought we should have our turn to keep and take care of Lee. I don't have any time for drinking or drugs so I tolerated Lee and treated him okay but I never felt obligated to do so.

Anyways we kept Lee for awhile with us. His health began to fail him more so admitted him in a private nursing home close by to home. The caretaker at that facility was Mary Williams. What are the chances we would run into another lady by the same name as the Mary Williams who was my friend that died awhile back.

Lee's whole right side was paralyzed, but despite his paralysis he still had one working side and got violent with Mary and gave her several black eyes. She had enough of his mess and we were forced to find him another nursing home near Licking, Missouri where he lived until his death.

Bob had his twin brothers Homer and Omer. Then there was Bob's brother Raymond who was closer to my age. His brothers would always call Bob "R.B." His brothers looked down on Bob because he was a minister and they were about the opposite. Bob always tried to get them to go to church so they would never come to visit us, probably to avoid him with talking about church and stuff. We would always have to go visit them if we wanted to see any of them.

Later on in life, Raymond ended up dying around middle of 1995. Its funny that at this time I was married to my third husband and I worked at a place about 5 miles away from Bob's brothers for almost two years and they never even knew it. I was never close to them when I was married to Bob so why be close with them now when I wasn't.

Bob only had the one sister Dorothy who came to visit us while we lived in Big Springs, Missouri. She lived in Portland Oregon so it was no short trip for her when she came to see us. Unlike her brothers she didn't mind that Bob was a minister.

CHAPTER SIX:
NO MORE PREACHER'S WIFE

I was so tired of moving around from school to school and church to church so while in Bowling Green Bob and I split up. The divorce pretty much ended Bob's career in ministry, at least in the churches. The church congregation will really judge a preacher's credibility if his own house is not in order. So he had taken a teaching position at the prison in Moberly, Missouri and moved to that area, about an hour or so away from me. We had bought a double wide trailer from the Sullivans so me and Phil lived in it for awhile. Bobby had already gone off to college and Phil was in his teens now. It wasn't a good time but I had enough of Bob's control over me and being so possessive. It had to end.

Life After Lockup

For the first time in my life I felt free. No man controlling me, whether it was my Dad or ex-husband. It was as if I got released from prison. Not too long after enjoying my freedom I met a cowboy, Les. At the time I was managing a Quick shop in Bowling Green and he began to stop by there on a regular basis to fill up his tank with gas and to come inside to chat with me.

From our conversations I learned that Les was in a middle of getting divorce from wife number two. Eventually we began dating. He made me think I was the most beautiful woman on the planet. We became increasingly serious and I thought it may be a good idea for us to move in together but no, Les wanted to marry me. So I became his third wife. Yet again I seemed to have jumped from the frying pan into the fire.

I got rid of my mobile home and moved to Louisiana, Missouri out in the country at one of the two farms Les owned. His nice house was located high atop a hill overlooking his farm and neighboring farms. Such a beautiful place roaming with horses. Indeed it felt good to be settled down but not without some drama I guess I should have expected.

My baby boy Phil moved in with us at the time. He was finishing up his third year in high school. He was such a good student in high school. While in high school Phil had also joined a martial arts academy, I think it was Taekwondo. He said it was a lot of kicking. I remember him getting his different belts and winning tournaments and such.

Well, there seemed to be growing friction between Les and Phil. My boy just blunt out resented Les and got to a boiling point one morning. Without going into details he ended up moving into his Dad's place at Moberly, Missouri. Phil finished out his last year of high school in that area.

Its funny cause Phil was nominated "Who's Who Among American High School Students" by the two different high schools he attended. He only had to complete a couple of classes his last year in high school to graduate so he also completed his first year of college at Moberly Junior College. Both my boys were so special. Phil ended up getting an art scholarship and went off to attend college at Springfield, Missouri.

It was just Les and me now out on the farm. His son was married and lived on a farm close to his so they would practice with their cutting horses a lot. They ran around the country competing in rodeos and his horses nationally ranked usually in the top three. I had a job cooking in a hospital at the time but Les cost me that job by complaining about me having to work on Saturday and Sundays sometimes.

Unfortunately, life is not without tragedies. It was now April 23, 1981 during Phil's second year of college when he received a note while he was in class to go to the college's administration office. They told him that his Dad had a heart attack so Phil immediately left school and drove about four hours to get back to Moberly. His Dad was in the hospital there.

Apparently, he had a massive heart attack while driving but was somehow able to walk through the hospital doors before collapsing. Bobby and Phil were at the hospital when their Dad died ten hours later. Bob held a prayer with his sons before his passing. I think he knew it was his time and wanted to make sure the boys would be okay. Both boys were so hurt, but I think Bobby was just devastated. I believe this is when he began drinking.

A year or so after Bob's death, I had been married to the cowboy for over three years now and my suspicions grew stronger about Les could be running around on me. One night I decided to drive over to his other farm about 30 miles away. I drove up the driveway and saw his truck parked in front of the farmhouse so I took my flashlight and walked quietly into the house. Low and behold there that S.O.B. was in bed with another woman. If I had a gun I would have shot them both dead. I was so so mad, the anger strangled my hurt. We were married for about three and a half years when we divorced over this incident. Needless to say I was just another notch in Les's belt.

It was 1982 and I had now moved into town to begin my new journey. I decided to lease a building and open up my own restaurant. Bobby returned home to help me out and Phil came back home when he was on college summer break. They were both truly the support I needed to get through this trying time.

I did really well with my new business considering what had happened. I made a good living that year. Not bragging but I am a pretty good cook. My restaurant became known for my pies in the entire county and business was booming. I am a survivor, always have been always will be. Despite what people say or think, I choose to decide my life on my terms.

Love of My Life

As time seemed to fly by my success flourished. I had hired a small staff and business was on the upside. A nice looking man began coming in for breakfast and then stopping by in the afternoons for pie and coffee. Brief chats at the cash register became longer conversations at the table where he ate. He would always sit at the same table in the back corner opposite from the restaurant entrance. His name was Louie.

Louie became very interested in me, but he told me that he was in the middle of getting a divorce from wife number two. Sounded a lot like my experience with Les so I was very cautious about picking up another man on the rebound, especially since this has happened with a couple of wives already. I was on the rebound myself with two past husbands.

Louie would ask me out on a date and I kept refusing for about six months. Then he assured me all of the paperwork had been completed for his divorce so one day I took off from work and went to St. Louis with him on our first date. He took me shopping and bought me a couple of beautiful outfits and then treated me to a wonderful dinner. Louie asked if I would want to go to a motel or head back home. We stayed at the motel.

Later on Louie asked me to travel down to Texas with him or a week while he looked for work. He was a mechanic by trade and a member of his Union Local 513 located at Bridgeton, Missouri. Anyways we had such a good time on the road together and our love grew stronger between us. For the first time I felt like he could actually be my soulmate, the one I was supposed to meet in life.

We moved in together and both had our reservations about marrying again. It was love at first sight for us when we gazed into each other's eyes the first day I saw him sit down at the corner table in my restaurant. We were perfectly happy to live together and didn't need to marry for now. I think Louie wanted to get married after his divorce was final but I really didn't care at that time. Nor did we care what our family or people in general thought about our choice.

Louie's union assigned him working at a rock job on the Mississippi river in the state of Louisiana. But he knew I would be worried about Phil if we were so far away. After the death of his Dad, Phil began to struggle through college. It was not an easy time for my baby boy. So Louie asked me if we wanted to bring Phil along with us down to Louisiana. Phil really liked how Louie treated me and accepted our invitation to head down south.

I really knew I had a good man and we ended up bringing my son along with us. I closed my restaurant and we moved down south. We bought a 35-foot Country Aire travel trailer, pulling it down with the pickup. We lived down in that trailer for four and a half years. After working on highway construction for awhile, Phil got a nice position as the groundskeeper at a big golf course. He was also taking college courses in the evenings and weekends.

The money was good but Louie worked such long hard hours. The summer months were especially tough with the high temperatures and humidity. In the meantime, Louie finally got his

Me and Louie, the love of my love.

divorce and we were married in 1984 on my Mom's Birthday December 28. Mom never approved us living together, she thought it was a disgrace to shack up. Every time I talked with her, two things she asked me, "Has Louie sold his farm yet and are you all married?"

Louie was so good to me. We never had an argument about anything. We had such a good marriage. But Louie showed increasing signs of emphysema probably due to him being a heavy smoker most of his life. When he coughed he had a rattle in the chest so time was running out on how much longer may be able to work so hard.

We had to move back to Missouri to get his retirement credits locked in with the union. I worked at Walmart so I went to their personnel department and checked on transferring to Missouri. I put in for a transfer to the Walmart store in Warrenton, Missouri which was in the union's area. It was a brand new store under construction so I was hired over the phone.

Louie's sister Anna Mae and her husband Darrell came to Louisiana and help us move back to Missouri. He was very close to his sister. This was around the same time Phil decided to join the Air Force. He flew off to Lackland Air Force Base in Texas for his basic military training.

So after Phil had left for Texas we packed up everything and moved back to Missouri. We decided we needed more space to live in than the fifth wheel trailer we had lived in while in Louisiana. So we rented a house so we could have a little more space to live. Louie went to work for Fred Weber out of the St. Louis area while I helped set up the new Walmart store in Warrenton.

The rental house owner Hank told Louie that we had too many vehicles parked at the rental house and we had to get rid of some. So while Hank and his wife Margaret were in Florida we found another place. We gave them notice and moved to a house located on a farm that was about 27 miles from Warrenton. So much more space with the house and surrounding land. No neighbors were close to us. No complaints about all our vehicles.

It was so peaceful and we had so much more privacy. Just a big difference from how we have been living in town and previously in Louisiana. It was farther for both of us to go to work but we had the freedom to do what we wanted. We planted a big garden there.

Phil in the Air Force.

Meanwhile Phil had taken some computer courses in college which helped him land a good job in the Air Force after his basic training. He ended up being a resource manager for the civil engineering squadron at Offutt Air Force Base located in Omaha Nebraska. After a couple of years the Air Force decided to civilianize his military job so he had to do something else. They didn't offer any Air Force jobs that Phil really wanted so he found his own job in the graphic arts field.

Phil standing by an outdoor display he painted for the Strategic Air Command at Offutt AFB in Omaha, Nebraska in 1987. He was in the Air Force but wearing civilian attire for an event.

He interviewed with the Air Force leadership in charge of that career field. There were no positions available for him but they liked my son's college portfolio and college computer coursework so much they created an extra position for him. His new career field was changing to computer graphics so his background was what they needed at the time. His command was the test base representing the entire Air Force for changing over to computer graphics and he ended up leading a task force to get it done.

Phil in the Air Force out on one of his military exercises playing war just like what he and his buddies did when they were kids.

While stationed at Offutt for a few years Phil met Shirley who was previously in the Air Force. I think she was an accountant or something of business at the main Post Office in Omaha when they met. If I remember right they met in the gym. Shirley was previously married with her son Tracy. It surprised us all when Phil told us she was black. They married and had my Grandson Phillip Robert Lamar Copeland in 1988,

Louie was so dead set against their marriage and never met Shirley. He was really against mixed marriages so I never felt he ever wanted to meet Shirley. She has treated me so good ever since they got married. Shirley has everything to do about sending me cards and gifts on all the special occasions.

Phil would just bring little Phil home several times just so I could see and enjoy my only Grandson. He was a beautiful baby. He was fair complected and had big dark eyes full of love. His hair was so pretty and was naturally straight. He looked so much like Phil.

However, when Phil visited us Louie did enjoy playing with little Phil, especially outside in the garden. I think Louie and me just came from another generation with old views. We had no issues with people of different races but we were raised by our parents to stay with our own.

Sometime earlier in 1988 I had some health problems. My blood sugar went high and I had a blocked artery to my heart. I had that fixed at the Missouri Baptist hospital in St. Louis. My boys came in for that. I got a handle on all my problems but had to go on disability. My left leg was now numb and I couldn't stand for eight hours to work a normal job.

Here is Louie with Bottom Star out at our farm in 1989.

The Social Security office turned me down twice for my disability application so I got a lawyer and won my case. It took me 14 months to win so I had both short-term and long-term disability during this time with my employer Walmart. I was in good shape and had an income.

In 1990 Louie was having trouble breathing so he stopped at the hospital emergency room in Lake Saint Louis and had some chest x-rays done. It showed a white spot which meant there was a tumor on one lung. So the doctor set up an appointment to have a biopsy done. It come up malignant and it was growing fast and would soon go into the esophagus which would shut the air off.

Louie decided on surgery at the St. Charles hospital and had the lung removed. My sisters Jean with her husband John and Grace with her husband Ray were there with me in the waiting room. There were complications during the surgery and it took over 12 hours.

The surgeon had some trouble. He was scraping some calcium off a main vein and it broke. They had to give Louie three pints of blood at this point. I was prepared to stay at the hospital. We didn't think he would get through the night so Jean and John stayed there with me. But he miraculously got better and I took him home. He was to start radiation treatments when he got stronger after the surgery.

When Louie started feeling better two tumors popped up so he had to start chemotherapy. That was a rough treatment. They had to keep him overnight at the hospital twice as he got very sick from the treatments. It wasn't like we were close to the hospital, we lived 55 miles away.

Louie's nephew Bob Smith and his wife Margaret came up to our house once or twice and stayed the night. I appreciated them so much. Since then Bob had died. He was a full blown diabetic. His sister Betty and Mother Pearl had both passed as well, both were diabetic. Betty and Pearl both had their legs amputated. They both lived in Rolla until their deaths.

Louie gradually became weaker and a couple of times he become so dehydrated that I had to admit him in the hospital. I took my suitcase with me and stayed in his hospital room every time he had to stay. The hospital treated me real good since they knew Louie was a terminal case.

Louie was a real macho man, being a construction worker. He had me give him all of his baths. He didn't want the nurses to do that. Once they wanted to bathe him in the intensive care unit and Louie told them that I didn't have anything to do and I would do it. I gave him every bath from day one.

Louie gradually got worse so I called Bobby and Phil to come home if they wanted to see him alive. They flew in on May 3rd and brought a new VCR thinking that would give Louie something interesting to watch. He didn't care about much of anything. The day the doctor told him he had cancer he gave up on living.

His daughter Debbie came to see him pretty often but his sons Mark, Dave and Jesse couldn't stand to see their Dad die. I stayed close to his side. I took a leave of absence from Walmart until Louie passed away on June 6th at 3:30 a.m. in St. Joseph hospital at St. Charles, Missouri. I called Debbie and then my sons first thing so my boys could make plans to come home again for the funeral.

Louie had been married twice, I was wife number three. So at his funeral both previous wives Virginia and Jo-Jo showed up. I buried him in St. Jude cemetery at Monroe City, Missouri. It is a Catholic cemetery but it is close to his people and I put a double monument up so unless there's a major change in my life I will also be buried there next to Louie.

After Louie died, my boys stayed with me for about a week. I lived in the country so they wanted me to move to town where I worked. I found a cute 2-bedroom house the day after Louie's funeral. We moved the things I needed and got me situated.

After I was settled in my new place my boys went back home. Phil was still in Nebraska and Bobby was now a music producer at Hollywood in California. Then my friend Shirley Young and I spent a week at my sisters in Marshfield, Missouri.

Shirley and Phil have the same birthday so they came up on the week of their birthday and stayed with me after I had settled into my new house. I made them this cake and also made Phil's cherry pie that was his favorite dessert. But only his favorite because of the way I made it.

Here I am standing next to one of the quilts I made for Shirley and Phil for their birthday. They loved all of the quilts I made for them over the years.

From left is my brother Wayne, my brother-in-law John (sister Jean's husband) and my nephew John Wesley (Jean's son). They are sitting around after eating lunch at our "Little" get together at my house in Warrenton.

My brother Glenn taking a snooze after we ate lunch.

From left is my niece Melody (Jean's daughter), Teresa and Stephanie (Ann's daughters) and my sister Jean.

CHAPTER SEVEN:
SINGLE AGAIN

Louie told me before he died that I needed to get out and find me another man. I was 53 years old when he died. He said that I was too young to stay alone. So about a year after his funeral I joined a singles in agriculture group. They were people from all over. I wrote some of the guys and met several.

Some glamour shots of me in 1994. Ready for the dating game.

The Dating Game

The group held a monthly meeting so I first wrote a Tom Jones and I messed around with him for awhile. I was still working for Walmart so I took him to our Christmas party. That didn't seem to last too long.

Then I met a Keith and he desperately needed a wife. He had four children and eight grandkids close by his place. Keith fixed Sunday dinner by himself for them and went to church too.

When he came to meet he had previously called me on Wednesday and said he was six feet tall.

Well anyways it was Saturday and Keith rang my doorbell. There he stood with a bunch of flowers and he was bald headed and short. Keith said, "I may not be tall enough for you." I replied that I wondered how he shrunk so much from Wednesday to Saturday. I was concerned he had a terrible disease. I saw him two or three times. This was in the middle of winter.

Keith called me for our second date and asked me if he came to pick me up from about a hundred miles from where he lived if I would like to stay the weekend. He wanted me to meet his family. He owned a service station uptown and had to work a half day on Saturday so while he was at work I was at his house fixing a turkey with all the trimmings and hot rolls, along with a pie and cake for his Sunday dinner.

The next day his kids really enjoyed my feast and thought their Mother had come back from the dead. He asked me after we ate how long he had to wait to ask me to marry him. I about swallowed my false teeth.

He had 35 old sows out on his farm and he said his wife delivered pigs while he was at work. She also did the garden and yard work. He even drove me by their local Walmart store and said, "You could work here." I let him come back to my house one more time and I broke it off with him at my house which was a big mistake. I liked to of never got rid of him.

Then I met a few more men. A George from Illinois told me over the phone that he couldn't have sex on the first date because he still had feelings for his late wife Betty. George came to my house in Warrenton and I had a motel room rented for him to stay. So the next morning I told him to come to my house and I'd fix him some breakfast.

George came by and I was cooking in the kitchen. He grabbed me and started rubbing on me. I pushed him away and asked, "What about Betty?" He said, "She will get over it." George was a dirty old man.

I about had the food ready and I turned around. There he stood naked as a Jay bird. All he had on was a cap. George said,

"You can play with it while I eat." I said, "You can eat and then hit the road." That was enough of that!

I continued trying to find a decent man and met John Garrison through the singles club. He was a millionaire who would bring me a lot of nice gifts. We dated for quite some time. However, John did have a living wife but he finally got a divorce from her. Come to find out he was seeing how many women he could find. I finally had enough and broke up with him.

After some time had passed I thought I would get out and try to find me another Mr. Right so I met up with a guy Norman Marriott. I think I saw his name in the paper and it said he was a non-smoker and non-drinker. He called me one night and asked me to come there. So I got there around midnight. Norman smelled like a brewery and also smoke. Men tell you what they want you to know.

This man was a moocher. He would load up with groceries every time he came to my house and meet. Then he would meet me at the bank in Springfield where I would cash my check and he would ask me for money there. But he did repair things for me such as my dishwasher and car. So I guess we were trading off favors

Norman was in charge over all the maintenance at a hospital in Eureka Springs, Arkansas but his work hours were cut so he probably needed to find ways to keep afloat. But he never told me why they cut his hours and I had my suspicions. I got fed up with his same old pattern. The only place he wanted to take me was to the bed. I ended that soon. The last time Norman came to my home I taped a Dear John letter on my front door. He took it and left.

Then an old flame, John Garrison, moved to town so we hooked up again. We took a trip to Florida together. He was a millionaire a couple of times over but I still paid for half the trip and he took my money. He took his little fat dog with us and he laid in the backseat while we drove down and back from the trip. The backseat got to smelling before we got back home. The dog got more attention than I did.

John loved his money and was always looking at the classified ads to try to find an old car to fix up and resell or a fixer upper house to repair and flip for a profit. That is essentially how he made all of his money. He would owner finance to people who had a bad credit record and charged them 12 to 14 percent interest rate. He took advantage of the fact his clients couldn't get a loan so he was able to make a ton of money off of them.

John was carrying around 20 deeds of trust which was over 1,000 acres of land. He was definitely one of these people who worshipped money. But, I'm afraid they are going to come up short when he had to face his maker some day. I have never seen a U-Haul behind a hearse yet and I doubt it will happen with John.

God has to come first in our lives. I have tried to help several people the last fifteen years. God takes care of me and He knows I will help those in need. The only thing I will need is a dress to wear when I leave this earth. All of our earthly possessions are just loaned to us to get by in this life until God calls us home.

CHAPTER EIGHT:
CARETAKER

Well to be honest up to this point in my life I have always been good at taking care of our family members. Everybody in our family always seemed to look at me to get stuff done under emergency situations. So why not do it for money. I started my new career taking care of elderly people in their homes. I had several good cases around Wentzville, Missouri. I worked for a lot of people in the Catholic church who were looking for good care for their Mothers. They all were good taking care of their Mothers. I worked for a couple in Florissant, Missouri. They all seemed to love me, both the guardians and the elderly people that I cared for.

Looking After the Elderly

In O'Fallon, Missouri took care of a lady they referred to as Aunt Nanie. She had a friend Barbara who was also her guardian. Aunt Nanie was a 100 years old. She had a leg that was swollen when I first reported for work. I immediately called Barbara and told her I thought she may have a blood clot. So she called the nurse over to check her.

After checking her condition the nurse had her taken to the hospital. Turned out Aunt Nanie was indeed diagnosed with a blood clot. At this time Barbara was very sick herself and couldn't go to the hospital so I volunteered to go. I stayed at the hospital for four or five days.

Barbara paid me all my wages and brought me fruit while I stayed with Aunt Nanie. She didn't take any medication except for one aspirin a day. She had been real healthy before this incident. The hospital sent her home in about a week and the blood clot moved. It went to the heart and killed her.

Then Barbara had a cousin over in Florissant, Missouri who had a husband with Alzheimer's and a broken hip so I went to work for them. I stayed there for a few months and then Barbara gave me a job at her real estate business. I started out as her receptionist but ended up showing display homes. She paid me well but I brought in quite a bit of new business for her. I worked Thursday through Sunday, two days by myself.

After awhile I had the urge to go back into caretaking. I found another job caring for an elderly lady. I really loved caring for the elderly sick people. I got a lot of satisfaction in knowing I was helping someone. My Dad told me before he passed away that I should go for nurses training but at that time I had two boys to raise and I wanted to give that my all.

After I finished caring for that elderly lady I moved to Marshfield, Missouri. I found a nice 2-bedroom duplex out in the country not too far from town. I decided to move there to be closer to my sisters Ann and Jean. Louie thought I should be near my people after he died. But that was one of the biggest mistakes I ever made. I didn't really know how my sisters got along until I had already moved.

Their bad relationship was caused a lot by their husbands. Ann married Dale and Jean married John. Dale and John are cousins and as boys they fought all through high school. The bad blood between them spilled over into their adult life. And the sisters inherited their husbands' feud. They lived within a few miles of each other but never spoke to one another at all. It was a chapter out of the Hatfield and McCoys. I could not believe my sisters and their husbands were behaving in such a manner.

I was taking care of an elderly couple, the wife was dying of cancer. While I was working there Shirley and Phil bought me a plane ticket to go visit them in Washington, D.C. for Thanksgiving. I had such a fun time and Shirley took me shopping in some uptown stores. She was a class act with good taste. I couldn't have had a better daughter-in-law.

The couple I was caring for liked me so much they were willing to hold my job. They just loved my cooking and how I treated them. But I couldn't stand to see somebody else die of cancer after I had gone through that with Louie. So while I was still visiting Shirley and Phil I called the elderly couple and gave my notice that I would not be returning.

When I returned home to Marshfield I placed an ad in the newspaper for my caretaking services and a lady Freda from

Elkland, Missouri called me. She was a widow. The doctor's wife had told me that the husband killed himself. Freda tried to be mean and hard to work for but I ignored her.

Before I went to work for Freda she gave Daren, a great nephew of hers, 30 acres of land and put a nice trailer on it for him. She thought he would help her, but he never called or came by unless he wanted something from her.

Daren talked her into giving him some papers for a plot of the farmland that he rented out for the hay. He just never treated Freda right. Daren married and had a son, then they divorced. His wife took the boy. Then he married again and had a daughter.

While I was taking care of Freda I had befriended Jennifer who had bought a house across the road from Freda. I liked Jen and showed her how to cook some of my special foods. I also gave her a quilt I made for her. She really loved it and struggled with the idea of using it or to hang it on the wall for display. Jen called it a piece of art.

Jen was 52 years old and was dating George who was 88 years old. They were both originally from Springfield, Missouri. He was a devout Catholic. They had been dating for awhile and she put the squeeze on him and told him she couldn't sleep with him until they got married. Jen and George had set a wedding date.

I was invited but I didn't go. Freda went and said George had on a new pair of slacks with the bottom of the legs turned up. I guess they didn't have time to hem them. She said Jen looked nice. George had two sons. One approved their marriage and one didn't.

So anyways Jen was an animal lover. Any animal anybody had to give away she would take it. She had twelve dogs and about fifteen cats when they moved in together. Their house was located on a busy highway so several of the animals got killed in traffic. It kept poor George busy digging graves and mourning over all of them.

Oh yeh and they also had two pot belly pigs, Romeo and Juliet. They looked like ark razor backs. The pigs were old and ugly. Romeo got busy and got Juliet pregnant and she popped out a couple more pot belly pigs. One day Juliet ran away from home.

The neighbor found Juliet and brought her back home to Jen and George. Then Juliet left home again and was never to be found again. I guess she got tired of the family life.

Then awhile later low and behold Romeo got out of his pen. He came across the highway with his big belly dragging on the pavement. He got under one of Freda's big shrubs and spent the night there. The next day Jen came to pick him up and drove him back to her house. Then again Romeo got out and never came back home.

By this time Jen had bought twenty horses and mules, goats, rabbits, chickens, more dogs and more cats. Jen and George's place looked like animal paradise. They only had ten acres and much of the land was occupied with farm and machinery sheds.

Jennifer would attend a Methodist church every Sunday and George being a Catholic stayed home. He would go across the road and chat with Freda and me. So after it stopped raining one early morning in the summer before the sun came up Jen went out to start feeding the animals.

George had a bad heart so he would just stay in the house while she fed all the animals. After she was done around 5 in the morning Jen called over to Freda and asked me to come over to see if her husband was dead. I went over to check and he was very dead. I called the Catholic priest and he wouldn't come out since George was already dead. Then I called the funeral director from Springfield who came and took away the body.

Jen really missed George. She met a couple Time and Lisa through a horse sale. They became good friends and they eventually took possession of Jen's farm. So Jen left her farm in style and had a big ole pig cook out. She had the food catered in for this big outdoor event. There were a lot of folks there, but I think there were even more cats and dogs.

Jen had like over 25 cats and over 30 dogs running around the place. What was suppose to be a festive occasion ended up in a big mess. All the cats and dogs were up on the tables and enjoying the feast and it just became a real mess. Freda didn't feel like coming over to the party and that was a good thing given the disaster that happened. I managed to bring Freda over some food that the animals didn't devour.

Jen moved into Buffalo and not long after met another man Rascal. He was half George's age, in his forties. I think she liked how much of a rascal he was and the name was fitting for him. It wasn't too long until she remarried. She seemed very happy and Rascal had the energy to keep up with Jen.

Freda had a friend Fern who lived in uptown Elkland. They were friends one day and then they would spat awhile and then friends again the next day. This was a regular thing with them. A love hate friendship I suppose. Fern was old as the hills and had diabetes. Her hubby Audie was older than old as the hills, but that old goat still worked at the livestock auction every day.

Fern was a tight wad with money. She paid me $5 to take her to Springfield one day and then had her 54-inch television worked on and paid $400 for the repair. I never took her any where else after that. Her husband Audie had mental problems, probably spiritual. They had admitted him in a ward at some crazy house in Springfield for awhile.

When he was dismissed from there they packed his suitcase with somebody else's pajamas. So Freda had me drive her back to the crazy house to swap the pajamas. We went inside and there was a man down on the floor calling for Sarah. He crawled under the table. I don't know if his wife was named Sarah or if he was calling for his cat or dog. No matter who Sarah was, this man's mind had gone bye bye.

Well anyways back to Freda. She had a little dog Dinky. He was real smart. Freda gave him a big blanket and he would pull it and cover himself up. He would sleep on the floor in her bedroom. Dinky began having both kinds of accidents in the house and the carpet looked awful. Finally she decided we should take him to the vet.

They said he had heart trouble and put him on some pills. Dinky got better for awhile and then one day he got so weak that he drug himself up the hallway and into my bedroom. I told Freda she better call the vet and have him put to sleep. She called the vet out but was very reluctant. It was like pulling the plug.

Freda finally decided it was time so she had me get a trash bag and Rusty put Dinky in it. She had us wrap his blue blanket around him before placing him in the bag. I had to put a tie on the bag so dirt wouldn't get in his face when he was buried. We called Tom the lawn man to dig a grave in Freda's backyard.

This was in hot August so the ground was like concrete. He couldn't dig the hole by hand so he went home and got his tractor and post hole digger and got it dug. After he got the job done we went out to see. Freda didn't like the brown dirt look so I went to Buffalo and bought a bag of potting soil and fixed the grave up for her.

She also had roses in bloom and I made a bouquet and placed it on Dinky's grave. Freda mourned a least a month. She had no children and couldn't get along with any of her family so she turned to a dog for satisfaction and he was now gone.

Then there was a lawyer who came into Freda's world. His name was Jim and he was half Freda's age, around 46. She was in love with him and bought him a brand new car for him to drive around. Freda took him to Bennet Springs around Lebanon, Missouri twice a year. Jim drew up her will and they bought cattle together.

Jim would come out to see Freda on the regular and she liked just looking at him. Freda bought him all kinds of furniture and lavished him with clothes and jewelry. Jim had been married twice and had two live-ins. There weren't any children so Freda always thought Jim was sterile but never had the nerve to ask him. So she died not knowing.

It was now about three months since her dog Dinky had died and Freda was always getting medicine from her Dr.Tommay. I remember the doctor's wife telling me how much the office dread seeing Freda and her late husband coming in. They would just start fighting right there around all the patients. They brought a lot of stress and drama into a place that was suppose to help heal people not make them feel worse.

Anyways Freda had a lot of health issues. I was with her the evening she passed away. Freda hurt between her shoulders and I knew she was having a heart attack. It happened quick and she died on her couch. I first called the authorities and then I called Jen who used to live across the street and she drove right over from town. I also called another former neighbor Nadine who also previously took care of Freda. And then I called Freda's administrator who lived in Springfield.

When Nadine got there she called Freda's brother Elvin, nephew Darel, great nephew Daren, and her boy toy lawyer Jim. Without delay they all came over. Freda's brother immediately wanted to know who had the key to the safe deposit box containing her will.

The funeral director had just left with the body. So Jen, Nadine and I started cleaning stuff up around the house. Freda had a cabinet full of pills and meds so I emptied them into a five gallon bucket. Filled it up to the top. While we were being useful, the family members and Jim were thrashing it out about the safe deposit box. Nobody seemed to know where the key was.

So after trying to open it by banging it with a hammer and throwing it around they took the box to the bank so they could drill into it and get the will. Freda had left the 250-acre estate with her enormous brick house to Jim the lawyer. The family members were outraged. Her brother Elvin called Jim all sorts of bad names. But from what Freda had previously told me, Elvin ran around with all sorts of women so he had no right to judge.

Jim the lawyer made some things go through probate which included the car that Freda gave Elvin. Jim did this out of spite because of all the names Elvin called Jim. Freda left me a $30,000 CD but nobody cussed me out. However, from my conversations with her I think Freda wanted to change her will and leave me more.

Her family really loved how well I took care of Freda and they all knew how hard she could be to get along with. I ended up taking care of Freda for four and half years. She fired me twice while I worked for her mean self. Freda tried to control me, but I was not the one. I was with her when she had her big heart attack and died.

I called a lot of people that Freda knew. They included a former pastor Tom who now lived in Ohio, Bobby Fletcher in

Lebanon, and a friend Winston in Columbia. They all showed up at her funeral held in the chapel at Buffalo, Missouri.

It was surprisingly a pretty large crowd despite that many of the neighbors that attended didn't really like Freda all that much. Two of the pall bearers were just wearing jeans and short sleeve shirts. Another pall bearer had on a leather jacket. Two of them had on jeans with flannel shirts. There was only one who wore a suit. It was quite the comical looking group of pall bearers.

After all of this fiasco I needed a sabbatical and took a break from caregiving for awhile.

Then I went to work for an 84 year old man uptown. His name was Herman and he was one crazy old man. He tried to get me in the bed with him. Herman had Alzheimer's and smoked constantly. I told him I didn't sleep with people I worked for. I fixed him breakfast and lunch, would clean up and then go home each day.

I got tired of his talk. Herman talked religion the first two weeks I worked for him. But after that he talked about sex, sex, and sex. I wasn't having any of that. I called his son and told him to write me my check and I was gone. His son ended up putting that old gizzard into a nursing home and there he died.

While I was living in Marshfield Ann's daughter Stephanie was a real problem. She was an alcoholic. Stephanie and her husband had a child together but eventually they split up. Then Stephanie started dating a black man and it wasn't too long before she got pregnant. He was on drugs and her drinking was out of control. Miraculously she had a healthy baby boy. He was so cute and adorable.

Unfortunately, the Division of Family Services stepped in and took the baby boy away from their care. They were determined to be unfit parents. Family Services placed the baby in foster care. This resulted in the worse nightmare. Family Services didn't find out until it was too late that the foster dad was prejudice and he had shaken the baby so hard that he ended up in the hospital emergency room. In hindsight I wished I would have contacted Shirley and Phil about what was happening. They would have probably found a way to foster the baby themselves.

This precious baby boy had Shaken Baby Syndrome and was on life support. I went to the hospital to see what the situation was. The optometrist came in while I was there so I asked him if he could tell me what he saw. The doctor said, "One retina was detached and the other one was dangling." He died a few days later. I cry as I write about this tragedy.

Anyways the people whom I was working for in Springfield asked me if they could in anyway help, so I went to a bank in Springfield to set up an account for the baby and I also had my account at Empire bank in Marshfield that folks could send money to help out with any expenses from this tragedy.

It was now winter time in January and Stephanie was not on the street. I took her to Gordmans to buy her a coat, cap and boots. Later on she called me one evening. Stephanie was in a motel north of town in Springfield. So I went there to see how she was holding up. She had her bottle but needed some cigarettes so I gave her some money for that and some food. After I did it I wished I wouldn't have given her the money. I didn't like the fact that I had to drive around so late at night. She pulled this stunt several times.

Then Stephanie asked me if I would get her an apartment. So we looked. She was sick a lot so I paid a deposit and one month rent down on an apartment for her. At least I was able to get her off the streets. I had no choice, my good conscience did not allow me to just ignore my niece or pretend nothing was wrong.

However, it upset her parents Ann and Dale. Dale went ballistic on me and called me a bitch and a whore. He said Stephanie and I was both alike. I couldn't believe the foul stench coming out of his mouth and Ann didn't say a word.

I had previously put a freezer in their garage and filled it full of meat. Ann also had my pressure cooker over at their place. But after what just happened I just left it all there, dismissed it. I didn't tell my boys about what took place or they would have gone ballistic on Dale.

But things seem to go back around on folks that don't do right. Later on Dale got hurt on the job, broke his ankle. I ended up going to the hospital and took him home in my car. Then I went to the grocery store and bought them $277 worth of groceries and took it out to them.

Dale worked at his family-owned grocery store mainly stocking shelves and carrying out groceries. He really controlled Ann and she let him. Ann couldn't put gas in the old truck she drove. Dale took it to town and put $7 worth of gas in it a week. He wouldn't let her wear jeans, but he sure could gaze at the ladies when he carried their groceries out to their vehicles.

The only job Ann ever did was clean houses. But she mostly kept that bar shining for "The King" when he came home from work. Ann made me feel sorry for them. I bought them a new bed spread and curtains to match and mini blinds for two of their bedrooms.

Then there is my youngest sister Jean. She was quite the opposite of Ann. Jean got out and started her own insurance business in Marshfield. She let money go to her head. When John Wesley graduated from college and went to work for the CDC in Colorado Jean asked me to take his place in her office. So I started working for my little sister. She paid me $7 an hour which was fine but she didn't give me many hours to work so I took a job elsewhere in Springfield as a caregiver for an elderly lady, Minnie Leach.

Her and her husband were pretty wealthy. They had over ten million dollars and a 15-room house. Their home was full of beautiful antique furniture. The whole place looked much like a museum. They never had any children. But they did have nieces and nephews Betty, Randy, Mike and Bill. I went to stay at Minnie's house for work Sunday evening and came back home on Friday.

She paid me $85 a day and $10 a day for food while I was at her home. I also drove her white Lincoln Continental all over the place. When I first started working for her she had sores on both her legs. Her and her husband owned the Buffalo, Missouri Newspaper and she stood at a paper press and had poor circulation. Her legs appeared in pretty bad shape.

We ended up going to the burn center to a specialist and he showed me how to take care of her legs. The specialist said

Minnie needed support hose, tight ones. They were hard to get on her but I had to do what the doctor prescribed. It took six months for her legs to recover. On our last trip to the doctor, he told me to reach around and give myself a pat on the back. He said I did such a good job getting her legs well.

I probably could have been an RN. But I did work several years taking care of the elderly and that was something to the same level as far as I was concerned. I truly enjoyed helping others.

Minnie liked my work there and then one day she fell in her bathroom and broke her pelvis bone. That put her in the hospital. I was by her side the entire time in the hospital including in the intensive care unit. She was so grateful to me.

Then there was another lady Elsie Crump who I looked after. She lived in Marshfield. Elsie was known as the witch in that town but I thought I could handle her. Well wrong again. The first day on that job was to get her funeral clothes in a box and label it. I got that done.

Elsie lived in a 3-bedroom house and one of those rooms was full of groceries. I guess she was getting ready for a famine. I got a box of Jello and was stirring it up in a bowl. But it was so old that the Jello wouldn't gel. And then there were bugs in the cereal boxes, oh what a mess. She had two freezers full of stuff that was probably from the ice age. Sometimes I would try to eat there but most the time I preferred not to. The food was so old it would probably kill a dog.

Elsie had some old jewelry and she had me drive her to Springfield and went all over the place at different jewelry stores to see how much it was worth. Nobody wanted to even look at it, the jewelry looked like something you would buy at a five and dime store.

Elsie told me when she hired me that she had a lady to do the housework so I didn't do that work until one day she saw me siting there making a quilt. Everywhere I have worked as a caregiver I would sew quilts. Elsie thought I had too much time on my hands so she insisted that I clean the room I was staying in while I was there. I reminded her that housework was not part of the job and she needed to just get over it.

As part of the job I would go grocery shopping but Elsie would never send me to the store. She always called up the store and had them deliver her groceries. It was usually a school kid dropping off the groceries. They would always talk to me and Elsie would get upset about it and say to the kid, "I am the one paying you."

I remember a time that a week of work passed and it was the day before my payday and I needed some cash. I asked if she could pay me a day early and she refused. So I had to go make a special drive to the bank and get some money out of my savings account. She was adding fuel to the fire by acting mean in other ways as well so I began taking my things out of her house and back to my home.

Elsie was an Eastern Star lady. I think she thought she was going to heaven in her fraternal lodge. The Order of the Eastern Star is the largest fraternal organization in the world whose members are both women and men. Their members are suppose to have high moral standards based on charity, truth and loving kindness. Those are definitely things Elsie did not display.

Her son John died in his sixties from lung cancer. I'm not sure if that is part of the reason she acts so mean. But probably not. I think she is just naturally gifted being a bitch and has such a real talent to make folks angry.

So one day we woke up and Elsie informed me we were not cooking that day. We were going to clean out the refrigerator. It was full of cantaloupe, melon, tomatoes, boiled eggs and hot dogs she had boiled a week ago. She was so frugal and ignored expiration dates on the food.

Elsie was all stooped over and would look up at folks with her mean conniving look. She scooted around with her walker and always reminding me about things to do that I was already doing. The longer I stayed there the worse she got. I had enough of her crap so I packed up my things and was about to leave.

She asked, "What am I suppose to do?" I replied, "You could start being kinder to your help." I told her to pack her bags and go to Webco Nursing Home. The nurses there can just simply leave her room when she gets mean there. She stayed in that nursing facility for about five years until her death at 100 years old. She was definitely one of a kind.

CHAPTER NINE:
PROUD MOM AND GRANDMA

I love my boys Bobby and Phil so much. They are truly my main purpose in life. I felt I had no choice but to sacrifice anything necessary to do the right thing as a Mother should do. But my sacrifices were well worth the many blessings I received from having my sons. I am just so proud of them both. They are so much alike and people always commented how they knew they were brothers even before they knew.

Hello Hollywood

I spent time with Bobby during Christmas of 1990 in Hollywood California. He was a big-time music producer and songwriter out there. One of his neighbors was Tim Allen who had the show "Home Improvement." His dog died and he came by asking Bobby if he could help bury his dog.

Just goes to show you that people are the same no matter their celebrity status. I had such a fun time while I was out there with my son. Bobby knew so many famous people out there. My son is such a delight to hang out with.

I think one of my favorite celebrities who Bobby knew was Lucille Ball. I loved to watch her shows all the time on television. She had the I Love Lucy show, The Lucy Show, the Here's Lucy show, and the one with Desi Arnaz.

I remember his thick Cuban accent on the I Love Lucy show. The show was such a success but it was the first show on television that showed an interracial couple so they caught a lot of heat. They were both brave pioneers facing the deep seeded racism around us.

In June of 2001, Bobby decided to pack up and leave Hollywood and headed to Bangkok for new opportunities. He had previously done work there but somebody made him a deal that he could not refuse. So off he went!

His music production company flourished with many different types of jobs such as music scores for movies and television sitcoms. He travelled around all over Asia, living in

Thailand, South Korea and China. Often flying around for different clients who were even in Saudi Arabia I think. My Bobby is so very smart, he can speak so many of the different languages.

Since a little boy, Bobby has been considered a musical prodigy.

Here is a view of San Fernando Valley while I visited Bobby.

Trip to Germany

When Phil was in the Air Force he got an assignment to Germany. He was a career military man and doing great things in service for our country. While living in Marshfield and taking a break from caretaking I decided to go see Phil and his family. I took along my nephew John Wesley who was Jean and John's son.

We flew out of the airport in Springfield, Missouri and headed for Memphis airport where we had to wait six hours to board a 767 jet destined for Europe. We flew 9 hours over the Atlantic ocean. The plane landed in Amsterdam and all of the people spoke Dutch so we felt pretty helpless. I couldn't even call Phil collect in Stuttgart to let him know what was going on. John Wesley called his Mom, my sister Jean to let them know what was happening and Phil knew that way.

We finally reached our destination, landing at the Stuttgart International Airport. Stuttgart was the capital of one of the German states there. Phil was there to greet us with open arms. It was so good to see my baby boy. Our luggage got lost so Phil was talking their language with them. I didn't understand any of the jibber jabber but my son was able to finally get our luggage

Phil lived in a vineyard area overlooking downtown Stuttgart. It was so beautiful to see and we would take strolls along the vineyard pathways and walk around downtown and enjoy all the restaurants and stores. John Wesley really enjoyed himself with little Phil. Shirley was such a great hostess and I love her to death. I couldn't have a better daughter-in-law.

Here is a nice silhouette of my Grandson Phil during our boat cruise down the Rhine River in Germany.

Phil took us to visit so many places all around Germany. We saw so many neat castles. We took an all day boat cruise down the Rhine River and saw so many different landscapes, castles and monuments. It was so much fun. Phil left his van at the place we boarded the boat so we had to take a train back from where the boat cruise ended.

It was really late at night and we were so tired. Nobody spoke English so Phil was talking jibber jabber with folks to find out the train schedule and buying the tickets. We finally got back to the van past midnight. Phil drove a van full of snoring people and got back home past 2 in the morning.

One of my favorite castles we visited was the one that Disney used for their castle. It was in Bavaria Germany. There was a very long bridge high up in the mountains that we walked across to get to the castle. It was very high and scary, but the surroundings were beautiful. What wonderful views. Little Phil and John Wesley had such a good time running around and such.

Shirley and Phil standing along the Rhine river in Germany.

The Black Forest was another trip that I really enjoyed. It was a mountainous region in southwest Germany, bordering France. There were dense, evergreen forests and picturesque villages. This area was often mentioned in fairy tales. I think Phil said they were known for their cuckoo clocks and grandfather clocks. They been making clocks in the region since the 1700s. We saw all kinds of Gothic buildings and walking around the many vineyards. I sure did get a lot of exercise while visiting Phil.

Good Times in Washington DC

My first trip to Washington DC was in 1995 when I flew out to visit Shirley and Phil for Christmas. He was still in the Air Force and working at a Department of Defense university. He previously was working for the Air Force Surgeon General. They were living on a big Army post and their house was located in a forest next to the Potomac river. The surrounding area was beautiful to look at, especially in the mornings with my cup of coffee walking along the river.

At this time Shirley had an important job under Secretary Ron Brown at the Department of Commerce. She worked closely with and were also good friends with Leola Roscoe Dellums who was the wife of Congressman Ron Dellums. She went by Roscoe. Very intelligent lady, a lawyer. Shirley took me to hang out with them and we all went to see the play "Cinderella" at a local theatre.

We went to eat after the play at some really uptown restaurant overlooking the Capitol. It felt like I was in a movie. It was so much fun. I am always so tickled about what Shirley does and who she knows. I am even more tickled about the love she displays to her family and how she treats me like a queen.

I have a memory embedded in my mind that still to this day makes me chuckle. It was Christmas Eve and we were all gathered around the Christmas tree with a whole bunch of presents underneath. I remember little Phil was gazing at all of them and mumbled that it wouldn't take him long at all to open all these up. I wasn't sure what he was talking about. I think he was around 7 years old. Anyways we all went to bed.

The next morning when we all went down to the living room there was wrapping paper and open boxes all over the floor. Just a mess everywhere. Well, I knew now what little Phil was talking about. Somehow in his mind all those presents were his and just decided to unwrap all of them before anybody else was awake yet. Oh my, poor Phil. After some lengthy scolding from both parents he was sent to his room.

I was feeling real warm as if I got in trouble too. The room temperature probably went from 70 to 150 degrees in a manner of minutes. It wasn't real funny at the time but we laughed about it later when the shock of it wore off the parents. Shirley and Phil were just outdone and in disbelief. It was the surprise that did not settle with them for sure.

Then I remember later when my son Phil was mentoring school students on his off-duty hours. He would walk from work to the place he tutored kids. One particular winter night I had their van and I was suppose to go pick up Phil where he tutored. My Grandson Phil was with me. Shirley was at some special conference for her work.

I drove around and was getting lost and little Phil said, "Oh no Grandma, we have to find my Dad before he freezes out there." He was so worried about his Dad. My Grandson was able to see where we were and told me how to get to where we needed to be. We got there and picked up his Dad and I had both my Phils now. I laugh a lot about this memory too.

I flew back out to Washington DC in 2006 for my Grandson's high school graduation. My son Phil at this time was retired from the Air Force since 2004. When he decided to get out of the military he was working at the Pentagon and in charge of their big Department of Defense website. They didn't want to lose him in this job so they made him a civilian job offer he couldn't refuse and that's how he became a federal government employee.

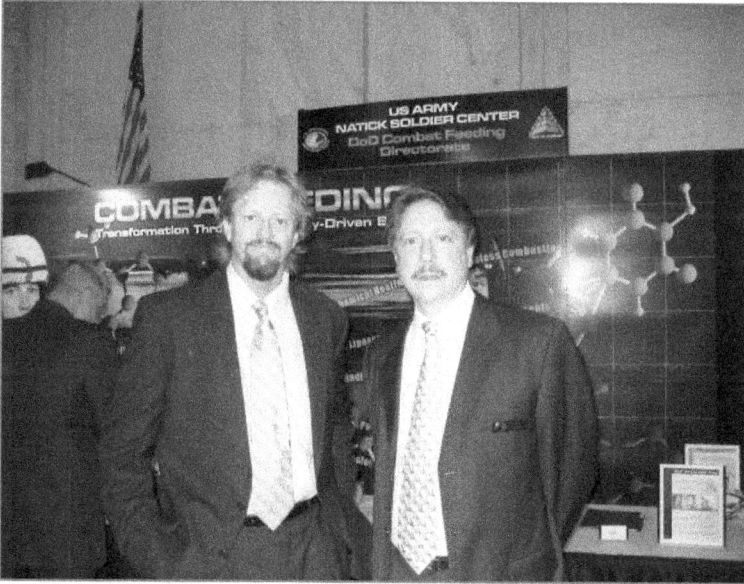

Phil (left) covering a news story at a Future Warrior Conference on Capitol Hill in August of 2004. He had just retired from the Air Force in April so I guess he decided to let his hair grow out.

Phil and family were living in a nice home in Virginia about 30 miles away from the Nation's Capital. Shirley did such a wonderful job decorating their home. She had an important high-level job with the Navy at this time. Shirley was a great Mother and a true leader wherever she worked. She was so smart and had impeccable style. I always enjoyed when she took me shopping or what gifts she got me.

Anyways I attended Phil's graduation that was held at a local university. There were so many people there and it was a wonderful event to see my tall handsome Grandson walking down the aisle and up onto the stage to receive his diploma. Thereafter Phil went off to college.

In 2009, My Daughter-in-Law Shirley at the White House for a meeting. This was during the President Obama administration.

Me with my Grandson Phil at his high school graduation.

Me enjoying a nice fresh cup of coffee on my 80th birthday. My son Phil took this picture of me sitting across the table when we were eating breakfast. He and my stepdaughter Debbie made the day so special with a huge surprise party all decorated in one of the event rooms at Webco Manor Nursing Home in Marshfield, Missouri.

EXTRA STUFF:
SOME MORE PHOTOS

Here are some more pictures I wanted to share.

Christmas at Washington, D.C. in 2011 with my family. They always make me feel so special and loved. The front row from the left is my step grandson Tracy's wife Latrice, my wonderful daughter-in-law Shirley (Phil's wife), my son Bobby, me, and Guy Jr. (my grandson Phil's brother-in-law). The back row from the left is my step grandson Tracy with his daughter Bella (my great step granddaughter), my son Phil, my grandson Phil, Guy and Cheri (my grandson Phil's in-laws), and my grandson Phil's wife Briona. Every Christmas we had together was much cherished.

Here is a cherry pie I cooked just for my son Phil at Christmas in 2011. That was always his favorite and he would only eat my cherry pie. Nobody else seemed to make it the way he liked it. My baby boy would sometimes eat about the whole pie in one sitting.

My Grandson Phil and Granddaughter-in-Law Briona visited me at Webco Manor nursing home in Marshfield, Missouri in June 2015. They drove all the way out from Washington, D.C. to see me. I can't express enough how that really touched my heart for him to do that for his Grandma. Also in this picture is my stepdaughter Debbie and her husband Mike with his brother Tom in the red shirt. Debbie is the daughter I always wanted in life.

www.ingramcontent.com/pod-product-compliance
Lightning Source LLC
Chambersburg PA
CBHW070015110426
42741CB00034B/1883